||||||| ||||| |||||||||
D0773851

NCE

Everyman CityMap Guides

Welcome to Florence!

This opening fold-out contains a general map of Florence to help you visualise the large districts discussed in this guide, and 4 pages of valuable information, handy tips and useful addresses.

Discover Florence through 6 districts and 6 maps

A Centro Storico
B Santa Maria Novella
C San Lorenzo
D Santa Croce
E Santo Spirito / San Frediano
San Miniato al Monte

For each district there is a double-page of addresses (restaurants – listed in descending order of price – pubs, bars, music venues and shops) followed by a fold-out map for the relevant area with the essential places to see (indicated on the map by a star ★). These places are by no means all that Florence has to offer but to us they are unmissable. The grid-referencing system (**A** B2) makes it easy for you to pinpoint addresses quickly on the map.

Transport and hotels in Florence

The last fold-out consists of a transport map and 4 pages of practical information that include a selection of hotels.

Thematic index

Lists all the sites and addresses featured in this guide.

SPECIALTIES

Ribollita: thick country soup made with bread and vegetables, boiled several times over and flavored with olive oil
Pappa al pomodoro: soup, bread and tomato
Trippa alla fiorentina: tripe with ham, tomatoes and parmesan
Fagioli all'uccelletto: haricot beans (tomato, onion and sage sauce)
Baccalà alla fiorentina: salted cod and vegetables
Tartufo: white truffle
Funghi porcini: cep mushrooms
Bistecca alla fiorentina: thick rib of beef, served grilled

BOBOLI GARDEN

PERINI'S CHEESE STALL AT THE MERCATO CENTRALE

Tel. 055 47 54 11
Police
→ Tel. 112/113
Lost property
→ *Via Circondaria, 19 (north of the station)*
Tel. 055 36 79 43
Mon-Sat 9am–noon

GETTING AROUND

The street numbering system in Florence can be confusing as there are two types of number: a number in red, or followed by the letter 'r' (for rosso), for stores, restaurants and companies; a blue or black number for private residences. Each system works independently: a red '6' can follow a black '14'.

EATING OUT

There are few 'foreign' restaurants as Florentines enjoy eating the local cuisine. They are fond of

eating out, so reservation is essential, particularly Friday and Saturday. Credit cards are not always accepted.
Opening times
→ *Mon-Sat 12.30–2.30pm, 7.30–11pm. Often closed on Sun and in Aug.*
Trattoria, ristorante...
There are several types of eaterie to suit all budgets.
Trattoria or *osteria*: for a simple and authentic Tuscan cuisine
Ristorante: the next category up in terms of price, style and choice
Enoteca: wine bar-restaurant
Pizzeria: for cheap and delicious Neapolitan pizzas
Vinai: type of bar where you choose your meal from a cabinet
Fiaschetteria: snacks and wine by the glass, at the counter
Extras
Most restaurants charge for bread and cover (*pane e coperto*: 1.50 € to 2 €) as

well as service (10–15%).
Meals
All over Italy, meals are comprised of *antipasti*, *primo piatto* (pasta, risotto or soup), *secondo piatto* (meat or fish), *contorni* (vegetables), as a side order, and *dolce* (desserts).
Tuscan antipasti
Mainly cooked meats and slices of toasted bread, which are also served as an apéritif.
Salame: sausage (with fennel: *finocchiona*)
Crostini di fegatini: toast with liver pâté
Bruschetta: slice of garlic bread, olive oil, *pesto*, tomatoes, anchovies
Prosciutto crudo: uncooked ham
Chianti
The most famous are the Brunello from Montalcino, the Vino Nobile from Montepulciano and the Chianti from Sangiovese vines. Carafe wines can be good.

FLORENTINE STYL

Romanesque
(11th–13th century)
Florentine Romanesqu continued to show the influence of the Roman style: stark, elegant geometric lines and decoration.
→ *Baptistery* (**A** B1)
→ *San Miniato al Monte* (**F** D3)
Gothic
(13th–14th century)
Introduction of Gothic elements (pointed arch slender pillars, high vaults). However, the forms remained horizo simple and flat.
→ *Campanile* (**A** B2)
→ *Orsanmichele* (**A** B3)
Renaissance
(15th–16th century)
Widespread and particularly artistic per inspired by the human movement. The ideas antiquity brought into with contemporary tas and circulated by mea of the printing houses favored a style of art th revolved around huma clearly defined space, the local hierarchical organization of decora elements (Brunellesch expressiveness in pai (Masaccio) or sculptu (Donatello). In all arts quest for perspective.
→ *Palazzo Strozzi* (**B** A
→ *San Lorenzo* (**C** A1)
Baroque
(17th century)
Exaggerated forms, introduction of the cu and expressiveness; a reaction to Mannerisn the Counter-Reformat
→ *San Gaetano* (**B** F3)
→ *Pontormo at Santa F* (**F** A1)

COSTA DE' MAGNOLI

CITY PROFILE

- Capital of Tuscany
- 373,575 inhabitants
- 948,000 inhabitants including the suburbs
- 9.4 million visitors per year
- 294,000 scooters
- 68 museums & 6,000 historic monuments

MARKETS IN FLORENCE

WWW.

Italian National Tourist Office, Cultural Institute, consulate etc.
→ enit.it → italcultny.org
→ italconsulnyc.org

Florence online:
→ firenze.net
→ mega.it
→ comune.firenze.it
→ weekendafirenze.com
→ itwg.it
→ turismo.toscana.it

Cyber centers
Webpuccino (**A** A1)
→ Via de' Conti, 22r
Pleasant cybercafé.
Internet Train (**A** A4)
→ Via Porta Rossa, 38r
The most central of the 18 Internet sites in this chain. Very useful.

FESTIVALS

March–April
Scoppio del Carro
→ Easter Sunday
Procession of a float pulled

by white oxen from the Prato to the Duomo, then ignited by a rocket. The resulting firework display determines whether the coming year's harvest will be good.

May
Festa del Grillo
→ Ascension Sunday
Spring festival at the Parco delle Cascine: children buy crickets then release them for luck.
Maggio Musicale
→ Teatro Comunale Corso Italia 16
Tel. 055 21 11 58/35 35
April 20–June 20
www.maggiofiorentino.com
The oldest Italian festival (1937) includes some wonderful programs: concerts, ballets, operas.
June
Calcio Storico Fiorentino
→ June 24, on the feast day of St John, in Piazza Santa Croce
Costumed final of calcio,

a type of medieval soccer that allowed the different districts and their teams to make their peace. Concert and fireworks in the Piazza della Signoria.
Summer
Estate Fiesolana
→ End June–end Aug
Tel. 055 597 83 08
Festival of opera at the Teatro Romano in Fiesole; events in Florence, at the church of Santo Stefano, the Anfiteatro in the Parco delle Cascine and at the Piazzale Michelangiolo.
September
La Rificolona
→ Sep 7
Festival of the Virgin: Florentines walk down the streets holding lanterns.
December
Festival del Popoli
→ First two weeks
Tel. 055 244 778
Alfieri Atelier (**D** C3)
Via dell'Ulivo, 6
Socially themed movies,

screened in their original language, shown in several movie theaters including the Alfieri Atelier.

TOURIST INFORMATION

Uffici di Informazioni turistiche Firenze
→ Via Cavour, 1r   (**C** B4)
Tel. 055 29 08 32 / 3
→ Piazza della Stazione, 4
Tel. 055 21 22 45   (**B** E2)
→ Borgo Santa Croce, 29r
Tel. 055 23 40 444   (**D** B4)
Codes
England/USA–Italy
→ 00 44/011 + area code including the 0 (i.e. 055 for Florence)
Italy–England/USA
→ 00 44/001 + area code + n° (without 0)
Useful numbers
Medical emergencies
→ Tel. 118 / 055 21 22 22
Tourist Medical Center
(**C** B1)
→ Via Lorenzo Il Magnifico, 5

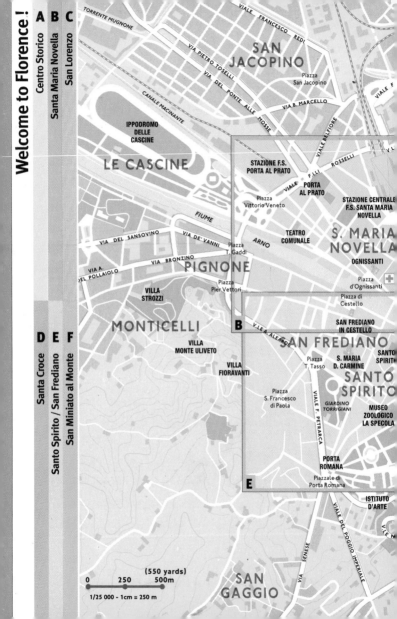

Welcome to Florence!

A Centro Storico
B Santa Maria Novella
C San Lorenzo

D Santa Croce
E Santo Spirito / San Frediano
F San Miniato al Monte

TORRENTE MUGNONE

VIALE FRANCESCO REDI

SAN JACOPINO

Piazza San Jacopino

VIA PIETRO TOSELLI

VIA DEL PONTE ALLE MOSSE

VIALE F

CANALE MACINANTE

VIA B. MARCELLO

VIALE BELFIORE

V. L

IPPODROMO DELLE CASCINE

STAZIONE F.S. PORTA AL PRATO

VIALE F.LLI ROSSELLI

PORTA AL PRATO

LE CASCINE

Piazza Vittorio Veneto

STAZIONE CENTRALE F.S. SANTA MARIA NOVELLA

FIUME

VIA DEL SANSOVINO

VIA DE' VANNI

ARNO

TEATRO COMUNALE

S. MARIA NOVELLA

Piazza T. Gaddi

OGNISSANTI

VIA A. DEL POLLAIOLO

VIA BRONZINO

PIGNONE

Piazza d'Ognissanti

VILLA STROZZI

Piazza Pier Vettori

Piazza di Cestello

MONTICELLI

B

V. LE A. ALEARDI

SAN FREDIANO IN CESTELLO

SAN FREDIANO

SANTO SPIRITO

VILLA MONTE ULIVETO

Piazza T. Tasso

S. MARIA D. CARMINE

VILLA FIORAVANTI

SANTO SPIRITO

Piazza S. Francesco di Paola

GIARDINO TORRIGIANI

VIALE F. PETRARCA

MUSEO ZOOLOGICO LA SPECOLA

PORTA ROMANA

Piazzale di Porta Romana

E

ISTITUTO D'ARTE

VIALE DEL POGGIO IMPERIALE

V. LE N

VIA SENESE

SAN GAGGIO

0   250   500m
(550 yards)

1/25 000 - 1cm = 250 m

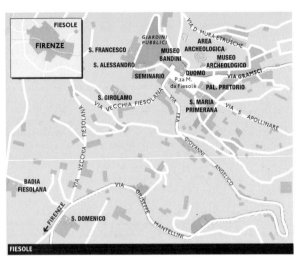

FIESOLE / Firenze

FIESOLE
FIRENZE
S. FRANCESCO
S. ALESSANDRO
GIARDINI PUBBLICI
VIA D. MURA ETRUSCHE
AREA ARCHEOLOGICA
MUSEO BANDINI
SEMINARIO
MUSEO ARCHEOLOGICO
DUOMO
VIA GRAMSCI
P.za M. da Fiesole
PAL. PRETORIO
S. GIROLAMO
VIA VECCHIA FIESOLANA
S. MARIA PRIMERANA
VIA S. APOLLINARE
VIA VECCHIA FIESOLANA
VIA FRA
GIOVANNI
ANGELICO
BADIA FIESOLANA
VIA
VIA GIUSEPPE MANTELLINI
FIRENZE
S. DOMENICO
FIESOLE

Mon-Sat 9am–7pm
Or 'Mercato del Porcellino', after the the bronze statue. Leather and souvenirs beneath the loggia.

Mercato delle Piante (**A** A3)
→ Via Pellicceria
Thu 8am–2pm (Sep–June)
Flower and plant market in front of the post office, beneath the porticos.

Mercato delle Cascine (**B** A2)
→ Via A. Lincoln
Tue 7am–1pm
On one bank of the Arno, everything under the sun.

Mercato di San Lorenzo (**C** A4)
→ Via dell'Ariento, Piazza San Lorenzo
Mon-Sat 8.30am–7pm
The best place for leather... try a little haggling. Belts, shoes, bags, clothes.

Mercato Centrale (**C** A4)
→ Piazza del Mercato
Mon-Sat 7am–2pm (and Sat 4–7pm, winter)

Attractive stands selling Tuscan products in a 19th-century covered market.

Mercato delle Cure (**C** E1)
→ Piazza delle Cure
Mon-Sat morning
The most authentic, some way out of the center in the residential district.

Mercato delle Pulci (**D** C3)
→ Piazza dei Ciompi
Mon-Sat 9am–7pm (and last Sun of the month)
Colorful flea market, held between the Loggia del Pesce and the pine trees.

Mercato Sant'Ambrogio (**D** D3)
→ Piazza Ghiberti
Mon-Sat 7am–1.30pm
The most interesting fruit and vegetable market within Florence's walls.

Mercato Santo Spirito (**E** D2)
→ Piazza Santo Spirito
Mon-Sat morning
Sells everything and, on the second Sun of the month, a flea market

(alternating with Ciompi or the Fortezza da Basso).

GREEN SPACES

Parco delle Cascine (**B** A2)
Two miles of rare trees, cafés, restaurants, tennis, swimming pool, a market, a hippodrome. At one end, there is a remarkable 19th-century Indian mausoleum.

Giardino dei Semplici (**C** C3)
→ Via P. A. Micheli, 3
Mon-Fri 9am–1pm
Founded in 1545 by Cosimo de Medici for medicinal purposes, this is the third oldest botanical garden in the world, with a cold house and a tropical house. The small park maintains its original layout and contains medical herbs.

Boboli Garden (**E** E3)
→ Daily 8.15am–7.30pm (4.30pm winter)
An oasis of greenery, with statues, on a hillside.

FURTHER AFIELD

Fiesole
→ Five miles northeast of Florence, with bus 7 from the station (30 mins); museums closed Tue; market Sat am
This village on a hill overlooking Florence is a delightful place for a stroll between villas and the fig trees, olive trees and cypresses. The bus stops in a square that affords a fine view of the city whose origins date back to Etruscan times: Teatro Romano, Museo Archeologico, Museo Bandini (Florentine art) and the Duomo. Breathtaking view from Sant' Alessandro; and, on the hilltop the Convento San Francesco. Walking back down along the Via Vecchia Fiesolana, stop at San Domenico (paintings by Fra Angelico) and the Badia Fiesolana (along the road on the right), a Benedictine abbey remodeled by Brunelleschi, with a cloister and a European university (superb view). Catch the bus back from San Domenico.

Certosa del Galluzzo
→ Four miles south, take bus 36 and 37 from the station. Daily 9am–noon, 3–6pm (5pm winter). Mass first Sun of the month at 11am. Guided tours.
Imposing monastic sites; a fortified Carthusian monastery, built in the 14th century on the orders of St Bruno: choir stalls, Renaissance cloister and frescos by Pontormo.

NTE VECCHIO AS SEEN FROM THE UFFIZI

CITY VIEWS

Piazzale Michelangiolo (F D2)
Good for an overall idea of the city's layout.
Forte di Belvedere (F A2)
A stunning 360° view of the area and grassy lawns for relaxing.
Campanile (A B2)
Bird's-eye view of the city, placing the Duomo within easy reach.
Palazzo Vecchio (A C4)
An unusual view of the city from the terrace.
Galleria degli Uffizi (A B5)
The café affords an unusual panoramic view of the Palazzo Vecchio and the Duomo.

affè

eligion in Italy.
resso: strong, black
fee in a small cup
ppuccino: with frothed
k and chocolate on top
a *latte*: milky
opio: double espresso
go: weak
cchiato: with a splash
ilk
retto: strong

SEUMS

ening times
Closed Mon or Tue and
an in the afternoon
t early in the morning to
id long queues.
servations
el. 055 29 48 83
visable in high season
the Uffizi, the Palazzo
i, San Marco, the
gello and the Galleria
'Accademia.
cessions
dents: when showing
rnational student card.

Museum passes
→ *The five museums in the Palazzo Pitti and Boboli Garden: 10.35 € (3 days)*
→ *Municipal galleries and museums: 5.15 € entitling the bearer to 50% reduction, valid for a year*
Free admission
EEC members under 18 and over 65.

CHURCHES

Mostly free entry. Coin-operated lighting.
Horaires
→ *Often 9am–noon, 4–7pm*
Dress code
Nothing above the knee.
Gregorian masses
San Miniato al Monte
→ *Winter: daily 4.30pm (vespers) and 5pm (mass); summer: 5.30pm and 6pm*
Duomo
→ *Sun 10.30am*
San Salvatore al Monte
→ *Sun 11am, 5pm (6pm summer)*

GUIDED TOURS

Various organizations offer tours with official guides (brochures available from tourist offices). They are ideal for getting to know the city quickly; also good for visiting museums in greater comfort with pre-booked tickets. Also available: coach trips through-out Tuscany or boat trips on the Arno river.

SHOWS

Listing from the tourist office
→ *in the bi-monthly Florence Concierge Information (hotels)*
→ *in the monthly Firenze Spettacolo (from newspaper stands) or on*
→ *www.firenzespettacolo.it*
Reservations
Box Office (**B** D2)
→ *Via Alamanni, 39*
Tel. 055 21 08 04

SHOPPING

Opening times
→ *Mon-Sat 9am–1pm and 3.30–7.30pm. Closed Mon ar (winter), Sat pm (summer), two-three weeks round Aug 15 Food stores closed Wed pm*
Sales
→ *End Jan and July*
Department stores
Coin (**A** B3)
→ *Via del Calzaiuoli, 56r and Via del Corso, 59r*
Tel. 055 28 05 31
Rinascente (**A** B3)
→ *Piazza della Repubblica, 1*
Tel. 055 21 87 65
Supermarkets
Standa (**D** B3)
→ *Via Pietrapiana, 42 / 44*
Tel. 055 234 78 56
Esselunga (**C** E1)
→ *Via Masaccio, 274 / 276*
Tel. 055 573 348

MARKETS

Mercato Nuovo (A B4)
→ *Via Por Santa Maria*

MUSEO DELL'OPERA DEL DUOMO

ORSANMICHELE

Piazzale de' Salterelli

Piazza S. Stefano

SANTO STEFANO

Piazza del Pesce

VIA DE' GIROLAMI

LUNG. D. ACCIAIUOLI

VIA POR SANTA MARIA

VICOLO DELL'ORO

VIA LAMBERTESCA

BORGO SANTI APOSTOLI

LUNG. D. ARCHIBUSIERI

DE' GEORGOFILI

LUNG. A. M. DE' MEDICI

PONTE VECCHIO

CORRIDOIO VASARIANO

FIUME

VIA DE' BARDI

ARNO

0   35   70 m

SANTA FELICITA   **A**

Piazza di Santa Maria Soprarno   **B**

5

6

★ Santa Maria del Fiore (Il Duomo) (A C1)
→ *Piazza del Duomo*
Tel. 055 230 28 85
Cathedral: Mon-Wed & Fri 10am–5pm; Sun & public hols 1.30–4.45pm; Thu & first Sat of the month 10am–3.30pm
Dome: Mon-Fri 8.30am–7pm (Sat 5pm)
Florentine and Renaissance landmark, and architectural masterpiece, built by Filippo Brunelleschi using neither supports nor scaffolding. When completed in 1436, it surpassed the domes of Pisa and Siena, both in terms of height (328 ft) and diameter (138 ft). At the top of the 463 steps, visitors can enjoy a 360° panoramic view over Florence. There is a spectacular *Last Judgment* fresco (1579) by Vasari and Zuccari inside the dome.

★ Campanile (A B2)
→ *Piazza del Duomo*
Tel. 055 230 28 85
Daily 8.30am–7.30pm (4.20pm Nov–March)
Graceful, free-standing bell tower, clad entirely in polychrome marble. It took 26 years of work and three architects to complete the campanile, begun by Giotto in 1334. Spectacular view of the nearby dome.

★ Battistero (A B1)
→ *Piazza di San Giovanni*
Tel. 055 230 28 85
Mon-Sat noon–6.30pm;
Sun 8.30am–1.30pm
This 5th-century baptistery, rebuilt in the 11th century, is another Renaissance gem, because of its bronze doors. The sculpted decoration of the south doors are by Andrea Pisano (14th century), while Ghiberti realized the north doors and the exquisite east doors (15th century), known as the Gate of Paradise (Old Testament).

★ Museo dell'Opera del Duomo (A D1)
→ *Piazza del Duomo, 9*
Tel. 055 264 72 87
Mon-Sat 9am–7.30pm; Sun and public hols 9am–2pm
Houses original works from the Duomo, Campanile and Baptistery that have removed for protec a must for Michela *Pietà*, the cantoria loft) by Luca Della R Donatello's *Mary M* medallions from the Campanile and the Baptistery doors.

★ Orsanmichele
→ *Via dell'Arte della Tel. 055 28 47 15 /Da noon, 4–6pm. Close last Mon of month. N Mon-Tue 9am, 10am Sat-Sun 9am–1pm*
This former grain m was converted into church in the 14th c There are fine statu patron saints of the in the wall niches a

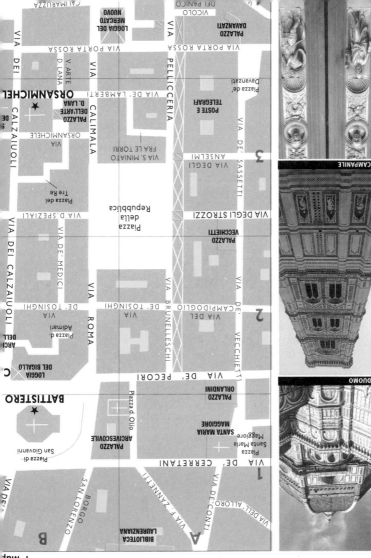

DUOMO

CAMPANILE

→ Map B

Centro Storico

↓ Map

A

Centro Storico

In the high season, Florence's historic center, the area between the Duomo and the Arno river, is packed with tourists, eager to soak up the city's incredibly rich artistic heritage. It was here, in the 14th and 15th centuries, that the Florentine merchants and bankers built ostentatious monuments as proof of their power, financing artists from Giotto to Michelangelo, who were to revolutionize Western art. Attractive pedestrianized streets, lined with luxury stores and stylish cafés, run between the cathedral, the Palazzo Vecchio and the Galleria degli Uffizi. On both sides, quieter medieval lanes reflect the original layout of the Roman city.

CANTINETTA DA VERRAZANO   PERCHÈ NO !

RESTAURANTS

Cantinetta da Verrazano (A B3)
→ *Via dei Tavolini, 18/20r*
Tel. 055 26 85 90
Mon-Sat 8am–9pm
This restaurant, which boasts an attractive traditional décor, serves a range of 100% homemade Tuscan dishes: *focaccia, panino tartufato* and cooked meats. There is seating near the wine cellar (fine Chianti) or you can stand, as people often do in Florence, near the bakery. *Focaccia* 2.30 €.

Giuliano (A C5)
→ *Via dei Neri, 74r*
Tel. 055 238 27 23
Tue-Sun noon–3pm, 5–9pm
Although this restaurant has limited seating, there is a cabinet of mouthwatering Tuscan dishes (soups, vegetables, roast meats), which are very reasonably priced. Choose the wine bar option opposite if you prefer to eat *crostini* at the counter with the regulars. Main dishes 5 €.

The Fusion Bar (A A5)
→ *Vicolo dell'Oro, 3*
Tel. 055 272 66 987
Tue-Fri 3pm–midnight, Sat-Sun 10am–midnight

The chef at the sushi bar in the ultra-stylish Ferragamo's Gallery Art Hotel is a student of the Shozan school, which subtly marries Japanese and Mediterranean cooking. Both the seating and the décor also show the influence of Japanese esthetics. Terrace on good days. À la carte 15 €.

Da Pennello (A C3)
→ *Via Dante Alighieri, 4r*
Tel. 055 29 48 48
Tue-Sat noon–3pm, 7pm–midnight
The attentive, meticulous service, delicious traditional cuisine and reasonable prices help you forget the crowds of tourists in this medieval district, which still recalls the Florence of Dante and Michelangelo. Menu 16 €.

La Posta (A A3)
→ *Via de' Lamberti, 20r*
Tel. 055 21 27 01
Daily lunchtime and evening. Closed Tue
Enjoy sophisticated Tuscan cuisine in the comfortable dining room of this former coaching inn. Fish specialties (*spaghetti di mare* 7 €). Plush surroundings and a pleasant terrace on a pedestrianized street. Large portions at prices to match. À la carte 30 €

ODEON

GIUBBE ROSSE

AL PORTICO

CAFÉS, ICE CREAM PARLORS

Perchè no! (A B3)
→ *Via dei Tavolini, 19r*
Tel. 055 239 89 69
Daily 10.30am–midnight
Tucked away in an old street in the city center, this modest-looking ice cream parlor has actually been in business since 1939. The homemade ice creams are full of natural ingredients: the pistachio and chocolate flavors are simply wonderful. Perchè no – why not indulge yourself indeed.

Gilli (A B2)
→ *Piazza d. Repubblica, 39r*
Tel. 055 21 38 96
Wed-Fri 7.30am–10pm;
Sat-Mon 7.30am–midnight
Belle Époque tearoom where the *signore* come to enjoy the excellent pastries, a house specialty since 1733. Beware, the cappuccino is expensive here.

Rivoire (A B4)
→ *Piazza della Signoria*
Tel. 055 21 44 12
Tue-Sun 8am–midnight
This confectioner is a Florentine institution, with an unbeatable location, a stone's throw from the Uffizi. But *the* thing about Rivoire is its deliciously thick hot chocolate.

BARS, MOVIES, CLUBS

I Fratellini (A B3)
→ *Via dei Cimatori, 38r*
Tel. 055 239 60 96
Daily 8am–8pm
Closed July–Aug
This tiny wine bar, dating from 1875, opens onto the street. Here you can put the world to rights with your neighbors, a glass of the best Chianti in one hand and a *panino* (roll) filled with *porchetta* or *pecorino* cheese in the other. Both 5 €.

Cinema Odeon (A A3)
→ *Via degli Anselmi*
Tel. 055 21 40 68
This Art Nouveau theater is one of the few movie houses that shows movies in their original language (Mon and Tue).

Giubbe Rosse (A A3)
→ *Piazza della Repubblica, 13/14r / Tel. 055 21 22 80*
Daily 8am–1am
Intellectuals and artists flock to this friendly literary café to enjoy an aperitif and, later, to hear specialist lectures. Works on the walls are a reminder that this was the birthplace of the Futurist movement (1909). Exhibitions of modern painters as well. Newspapers available.

Astor Caffè (A C1)
→ *Piazza del Duomo, 20r*
Tel. 055 239 90 90
Mon-Sat 10–3am;
Sun 5pm–3am
At the base of the dome, this café with its metal décor is the meeting place for a trendy crowd that comes here for an aperitif or an after-dinner drink. Concerts in the basement. Crowded at week ends, but friendly atmosphere. Internet access. Cocktails 5 €.

Yab (A A3)
→ *Via Sasseti, 5r*
Tel. 055 21 51 60
Daily 11pm–4am. Closed Sun and June–Aug
This ultra-fashionable nightclub holds themed evenings and boasts a great atmosphere thanks to good music played by established DJs: house on Tue and '80s hits on Wed. Admission and drink 10–15 €.

SHOPPING

Echo (A D2)
→ *Via dell'Oriolo, 37-41r*
Tel. 055 238 11 49
Mon-Sat 9am–7.30pm
Designed by an up-and-coming stylist, this line of womenswear is available in two stores, one casual, the other dressy. Very

reasonably priced.
Stefano Veneziani (A C3)
→ *Corso, 10r*
Tel. 055 21 41 13
Tue-Sat 10am–7pm;
Mon 3.30–7pm
This well-known men's fashion label inhabits one of the beautiful classic stores along the Corso: affordable Italian elegance.

Bizzarri (A C4)
→ *Via Condotta, 32r*
Mon-Fri 9.30am–1pm, 4–7.30pm; Sat 9.30am–1pm
Herbs, colored flasks and jars: the natural world reduced to powders and elixirs by a herbalist with a magic touch. They can be used for cooking, cosmetics, painting, photography, etc.

Al Portico (A C4)
→ *Piazza San Firenze, 1*
Tel. 055 21 37 16
/Mon-Sat 10am–7pm;
Sun 10am–1pm
A paradise of seeds, earthenware pots, plants and flowers.

Istituto Raffaele (A A4)
Via Porta Rossa, 12
Tel. 055 21 64 60
Mon-Sat 9am–7pm
Closed Sat pm and Mon am
Upmarket beauty treatments from pedicure to manicure in one of the salon's cozy cubicles. 13 –20 €.

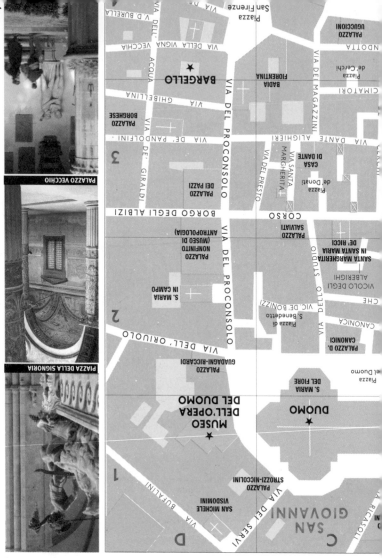

DI SAN FIRENZE

BORGO DE' GRECI

VIA DEI LEONI

VIA DEL CORNO

VIA DEL CORNO

D. PARLASCIO

VIA DE' MAGALOTTI

D. NINNA

VIA VINEGIA

VIA DE' RUSTICI

Piazza
San Remigio

5

LOGGIA
DEL GRANO

VIA DEI NERI

SAN REMIGIO

VIA DE' CASTELLANI

VIA CASTELLO D'ALTAFRONTE

VIA OSTERIA DEL GUANTO

SANTA
CROCE

VIA DE' BRACHE

VIA DEI NERI

VIA D. MOSCA

Piazza
de' Giudici

VIA DEI SAPONAI

VIA DEI VAGELLAI

ORIA

PALAZZO
DELLA CAMERA
DI COMMERCIO

Piazza
Mentana

VIA V. MALENCHINI

6

LUNGARNO GENERALE DIAZ

VIA DE' BENCI

C   D

**MUSEO DI STORIA
DELLA SCIENZA**

GALLERIA DEGLI UFFIZI

m above the church.
zza della Signoria

litical and civic hub
ence since the 13th
y is dominated by the
o Vecchio. Beside it
the Loggia dei Lanzi,
n see what amounts
mazing open-air
m of Renaissance
ure (with Cellini's
s).

azzo Vecchio (A C4)
zo della Signoria)
za della Signoria
; 276 82 24
ed, Fri-Sat 9am-7pm
Mon & Fri in summer);
d Sun 9am-2pm
litary air of the
built to house the

government in the 13th
century, gives no hint of
Vasari's lavish 16th-century
remodeling of the interior
for Cosimo I, glorifying the
Medici who founded the
Republic of Tuscany. The
walls and ceilings of the
Hall of the Five Hundred are
covered with frescos by
Vasari illustrating the theme
of victory over Pisa and
Siena.
★ **Bargello (A** D4)
→ *Via del Proconsolo, 4
Tel. 055 238 86 06
Daily 8.15am-1.50pm. Closed
1st, 3rd and 5th Sun, 2nd and
4th Mon of the month*
The leading museum of
major Renaissance works of
sculpture and ceramics:

Donatello, Michelangelo,
Verrochio, Brunelleschi.
★ **Museo di Storia della
Scienza (A** C6)
→ *Piazza de Giudici, 1
Tel. 055 239 88 76
Tue, Thu, Sat 9.30am-1pm;
Mon, Wed, Fri 2-5pm*
Besides other pieces of
scientific equipment, the
austere Palazzo Castellani
has the telescope with
which Galileo discovered
Jupiter's satellites.
★ **Galleria degli Uffizi
(A** B5)
→ *Piazzale degli Uffizi, 6
Tel. 055 238 86 51
Bookings on 055 29 48 83
Corridoio Vasariano by appt
only 055 265 43 21
Tue-Sun 8.30am-6.50pm*

(10pm Sat in summer).
Built by Vasari in 1560 to
house the administrative
offices (*uffizi*) of the State of
Tuscany, this became in 1581
under Francesco I de Medici
(1541–87), one of the
leading museums in the
world. It provides a remarkable overview of Italian
painting with works by the
country's greatest artists:
Botticelli, della Francesca,
Lippi, Michelangelo,
Pollaiuolo, Uccello, da Vinci,
as well as examples of
Germanic, Flemish and Dutch
work. Vasari's Corridor,
linking the Uffizi Gallery to
the Palazzo Pitti, offers an
unusual view of the Ponte
Vecchio and the Arno river.

Map L

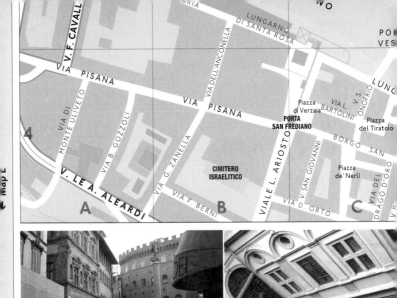

VIA TORNABUONI

PALAZZO STROZZI

★ Santa Maria Novella (B E3)
→ Piazza di S. Maria Novella
Tel. 055 21 59 18
Daily 9.30am–4.30pm; Fri &
Sun 1–4.30pm. Cloister:
daily 9am–2pm. Closed Fri
Santa Maria, near the
station, has a spectacular
Gothic-Renaissance façade
(Alberti, c. 1458). The rest
is older, in pure Florentine
Gothic style, inspired by
Cistercian architecture.
The church contains some
outstanding works: the
Trinity by Masaccio (dated
1427), the first experimen-
tal use of perspective in
painting, a crucifix carved
by Brunelleschi and one
painted by Giotto. Frescos

by Lippi and Ghirlandaio,
respectively in the Filippo
Strozzi and Tornabuoni
chapels.

★ Ognissanti (B D3)
→ Borgo Ognissanti, 42
Tel. 055 239 87 00
Church: daily 8am–noon,
4–7pm. Cenacolo: Mon, Tue,
Sat 9am–noon
This square lies at the heart
of a district of antique
dealers. In the 11th century,
this was where the
Benedictines developed
the woolen cloth industry,
bringing about the city's
expansion. The baroque
façade of the church
conceals a fine fresco by
Botticelli. Ghirlandaio's Last
Supper is in the refectory

(through the cloister).
★ Palazzo Corsini (B E4)
→ Lungarno Corsini, 10
By appt on 055 21 89 94
Entrance Via del Parione, 11
The finest residence on the
embankment, this palace
is a perfect example of
Florentine baroque. Its
terraces, adorned with
statues, overhang the Arno
river. At the top of the
sweeping staircase there
is a unique collection of
Florentine, Neapolitan and
Bolognese paintings.
★ Palazzo Rucellai (B E4)
→ Via della Vigna Nuova, 18
This elegant Renaissance
palace is closed to the
public. The façade (1446),
however, is worth a look

with its regular inter[
vertical pilasters ins
by Vitruvius' Rome:
example of Alberti's
★ Museo Marino
(B E3)
→ Via della Spada
Tel. 055 21 94 32
Daily 10am–5pm (1p.
Closed Tue and Aug
Modern in content a
presentation. One o
few museums in Flo
devoted to a 20th-ce
artist: Marino Marin
figure of Italian scul
★ Via Tornabuoni
The city's smartest
shopping street. All
names in Italian fas
can be found on thi
avenue, which stret

B

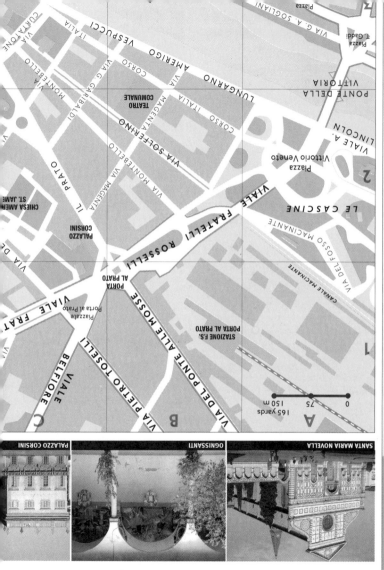

Santa Maria Novella is an essential part in the study and discovery of Renaissance Florence. Also, like Santa Trinità or Ognissanti, the imposing church contains some fine 15th-century scenes of Florentine life by Ghirlandaio. The district, stretching between the station in the north and the embassies and grand hotels in the southwest, is popular with visitors. To the west, Florentines flock to the Parco delle Cascine on Tuesdays for the market. In the east, around the Via Tornabuoni, the stately palaces are home to fashion houses. In the southeast, the Borgo Santi Apostoli and the Via delle Terme seem caught in a time warp, with their 13th-century fortified tower houses.

I' VINAINO

IL LATINI

RESTAURANTS

Tripes (B D3)
→ *Via M. Finiguerra, next to the Fulgor movie theater*
Daily 8–4am
One of those makeshift booths that perpetuate the working-class tradition of Florentine tripe. Craftsmen and businessmen share tables to devour intestines and other types of offal, any time of day or night. Portion 4 €.

I' Vinaino (B D3)
→ *Via Palazzuolo, 124r*
Tel. 055 29 22 87
Daily 10.30am–midnight Closed Sun
Good café with a regular clientele of local office-workers and shop assistants. Homemade dishes at unbeatable prices. Menu 8 €.

Trattoria Guelfa (B F1)
→ *Via Guelfa, 103r*
Tel. 055 21 33 06
Daily noon–2.30pm, 7–10.30pm. Closed Wed and Aug
Claudio, Alberto and Rosa are three good reasons to visit this restaurant near the station. Laid-back décor: paintings, old farm tools, tablecloths and paper napkins. Chicken in mushroom sauce is a specialty. Menu 8 €.

Il Latini (B E4)
→ *Via dei Palchetti, 6r*
Tel. 055 210 916
Tue-Sun lunch and evening
Rustic *trattoria* in the annexes of the Rucellai Palace. Always packed, and for good reasons: cooking is the vocation of the whole family, which serves up some excellent Tuscan dishes. Reservation essential (7.30pm or 9.30pm). À la carte 15 €–20 €.

Coco Lezzone (B E4)
→ *Via del Parioncino, 26r*
Tel. 055 28 71 78
Daily noon–2.30pm, 7–10.30pm. Closed Tue evening and Sun
This restaurant serves heavenly Tuscan cuisine. Chunky vegetable soup, meats served in rich sauces, artichokes in lemon. À la carte 20 €.

La Nandina (B F4)
→ *Borgo Santi Apostoli, 64*
Tel. 055 21 30 24 / Daily 12.30–3pm, 7.30–10.30pm Closed Mon lunch and Sun
Near the Via Tornabuoni, this restaurant provides an excellent cuisine in a traditional atmosphere. The *antipasti* and dessert are brought to your table on a trolley. *Pappa al pomodoro, ravioli tartufo*. Attentive service.
À la carte 20 €.

CCIA | BP STUDIO | ALICE ATELIER

CAFÉS

Rondinelli (B F3)
→ Via de'Rondinelli, 5r
Tel. 055 28 71 22.
Mon-Sat 7am-7pm
A local café, ideal for
a quick coffee or hot
chocolate in company
with Florentines who are
enjoying a snack of pasta
or salad at the counter or
sitting down.

Caffè Curtatone (B C3)
→ Borgo Ognissanti, 167r
Tel. 055 21 07 72
Wed-Mon 7am-1am
At breakfast time, the
Florentines cluster at
the counter to enjoy a
homemade pastry and
coffee. At lunch time, they
have a bowl of pasta and,
in the evening, a *negroni*
(Campari, gin and
Martini). Vaulted ceiling
and traditional frescos.

BARS, THEATERS, CLUBS

Procacci (B F3)
→ Via Tornabuoni, 64r
Tel. 055 21 16 56. Daily
10.30am-8pm. Closed Sun
This delicatessen is an
institution when it comes
to truffles. They are sold
fresh (Sep-Dec), in sauce
or as a sandwich filling
(1.30 €). Wonderful with
a glass of wine.

Capocaccia (B E4)
→ Lungarno Corsini, 12-14r
Tel. 055 21 07 51
Daily noon-2am
This bar, with its stylish
décor, is a popular place
to enjoy an aperitif:
unlimited substantial
crostini served with all
types of sauce and an
Italian bitter-based
cocktail (like Campari). In
winter, chart music at top
volume. In summer,
people sit beside the
Arno river. Delicious
cocktails 5-6 €.

Teatro Comunale (B B3)
→ Corso Italia, 16
Tel. 055 11 58/35 35. Tue-
Fri 10am-4.30pm (1pm Sat)
In May, this theater is the
seat of the Maggio
Musicale Fiorentino, one
of the oldest music
festivals in Europe, along
with Bayreuth and
Salzburg. It also stages
operas and ballets in the
fall and a symphonic
season in winter. This
venue has often made its
mark on the history of
music and stagecraft.
Fellini himself once made
a guest appearance here.

Meccano (B A2)
→ Viale degli Olmi, 1
(at the entrance to the
Parco delle Cascine)
Tel. 055 331 371
Tue, Thu-Sat 11pm-4am

Dance in the most
famous club in the city, a
popular night out for the
younger crowd. Mainly
the latest chart music.
In summer, there is an
open-air dance floor.
Admission 10 €.

SHOPPING

BP Studio (B F4)
→ Via della Vigna Nuova,
15r. Tel. 055 21 32 43
Mon 3-7.30pm;
Tue-Sat 10am-7.30pm
Ultra-creative fashions for
men and women in this
street lined with stores.
It's probably best not to
look too closely at the
price tags.

Exante (B F4)
→ Via della Vigna Nuova,
16r. Tel. 055 28 29 61
Mon 3-7.30pm;
Tue-Sat 9.30am-7.30pm
A wide selection of
leather bags by famous
and not so famous
designers. Bag 75-150 €.
If you like bright colors,
try Leoncini at n° 44r.

Le Stanze (B D3)
→ Borgo Ognissanti, 50-
52r. Tel. 055 28 89 21
Tue-Sat 10am-1pm, 3.30-
7.30pm; Mon 3.30-7.30pm
Dream décor: you'll want
to buy everything, from
furniture to crockery.
Italian design from the

1960s to the present day.
**Officina de Santa Maria
Novella (B** E3)
→ Via della Scala, 16r
Tel. 055 21 62 76
Daily 9.30am-7.30pm
Closed Sun, Nov, Jan-Feb
Founded in 1612, this is
one of the oldest and most
opulent pharmacies in
Europe. Something of a
museum; come just for a
look, or treat yourself to
something from the range
of essential oils, perfumes,
soaps or even sweets: the
Queen of England shops
here, so it must be special.

Alinari (B F2)
→ Largo Alinari, 15
Tel. 055 23 951
Mon-Fri 9am-1pm, 2-6pm;
Sat 9am-1pm, 3.30-7.30pm
Choose a fascinating
reproduction of forgotten
Florence from the ancient
photo collection dating
back to 1852. Contact
printing and a unique
collotype process.

Alice Atelier (B F2)
→ Via Faenza, 72r
Tel. 055 28 73 70
Daily 9am-1pm, 3.30-
7.30pm. Closed Sun
The carnival is no more,
but in this store the
technique of *papier mâché*
has been handed down
from father to daughter.
Artistic designs inspired
by the *commedia dell'arte*.

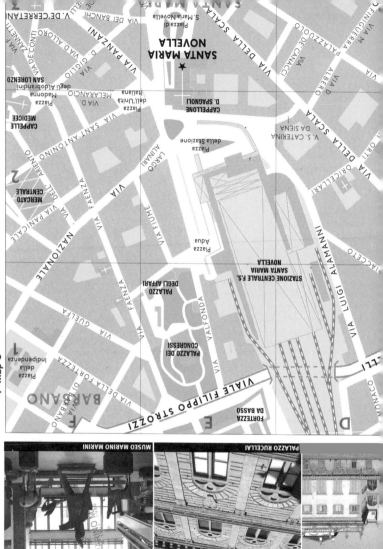

← Map C

SANTA MARIA NOVELLA ★

Piazza di
S. Maria Novella

VIA DELLA SCALA

VIA DEI BANCHI

V. DE' CERRETANI

VIA PANZANI

VIA D. ALLORO

VIA D. GIGLIO

SAN LORENZO

Piazza
Madonna
degli Aldobrandini

VIA D. MELARANCIO

Piazza
dell'Unità
Italiana

CAPPELLE MEDICEE

VIA SANT'ANTONINO

CAPPELLONE D. SPAGNOLI

V. S. CATERINA DA SIENA

Piazza
della Stazione

LARGO ALINARI

VIA DELLA SCALA

VIA ORICELLARI

MERCATO CENTRALE

VIA DELL'ARIENTO

VIA PANICALE

VIA FAENZA

VIA NAZIONALE

VIA FIUME

Piazza
Adua

STAZIONE CENTRALE F.S.
SANTA MARIA NOVELLA

VIA LUIGI ALAMANNI

JACCETTO

VIA GUELFA

VIA FAENZA

PALAZZO DEGLI AFFARI

VALFONDA

PALAZZO DEI CONGRESSI

VIA DELLA FORTEZZA

Piazza
della
Indipendenza

BARBANO

VIA DI BARBANO

VIALE FILIPPO STROZZI

FORTEZZA DA BASSO

MONACO

MUSEO MARINO MARINI

PALAZZO RUCELLAI

FERRAGAMO | SANTA TRINITÀ | PALAZZO DAVANZATI

e Piazza Antinori to
ta Trinità bridge.
stere Renaissance
belonging to the
Antinori family of
d owners forms a
contrast to the
aroque church of
etano. Nos 19, 16, 15,
and 3 are also worth
in the middle,
ctive early 20th-
loggia precedes
de of the Strozzi
To the left of the
column topped by
re of justice, stands
azzo Bartolini-
eni (16th century).
azzo Strozzi (B F4)
a Strozzi
239 85 63

Mon-Sat 8am–7pm
A perfect example of
Florentine Renaissance,
this palace was built for the
wealthy Filippo Strozzi by
Benedetto da Maiano and
Simone del Pollaiuolo ('Il
Cronaca'). The palace has
a monumental façade,
rusticated masonry and a
massive projecting cornice.
The inner courtyard is
completely enclosed, like
a small city within a city.
The palace is nowadays
used for art exhibitions
and fashions shows.
★ Santa Trinità (B F4)
→ Piazza di Santa Trinità
Tel. 055 21 69 12
Mon-Sat 8am–noon, 4–6pm;
Sun 4–6pm

The Mannerist façade of
this church conceals a
simple monastic interior
dating from the 11th–14th
centuries, which is highly
conducive to meditation.
Out of the shadows looms
the *Annunciation* by
Lorenzo Monaco (fourth
chapel on the right) and
works by Ghirlandaio
(chapel to the right of the
altar) which depict the
Piazza di Santa Trinità and
the city of Florence.
**★ Museo Ferragamo
(B** F4)
→ Via Tornabuoni, 2
Tel. 055 336 04 56
Mon-Fri 9am–1pm, 2–6pm
In the impressive medieval
Palazzo Spini-Ferroni,

above the stores of the
famous shoemaker
Ferragamo, is a museum
that exhibits some of the
extraordinary models worn
by various American stars.
**★ Palazzo Davanzati
(B** F4)
→ Via Porta Rossa, 9-13
Tel. 055 238 86 10
*Closed for restoration until
further notice*
On the edge of the
medieval district, this stark
medieval residence
displays a transitional
style, part-way between the
tower house of the Middle
Ages and the seigniorial
palace of the Renaissance.
Entering the palace is like
stepping back in time.

MUSEO DI SAN MARCO | GALLERIA DELL'ACCADEMIA | SPEDALE DEGLI INNOCE

★ **San Lorenzo** (**C** A4)
→ *Piazza San Lorenzo*
Tel. 055 21 66 34.
Church: Mon-Sat 10am–5pm
Biblioteca Laurenziana:
daily 8.30am–1.30pm.
Chapel of the Princes
(Cappella dei Principi): Tue-
Sun 8.15am– 5pm (1.50pm
public hols)
Behind the unfinished
façade is a wholly Renaissance church (1419–69).
Brunelleschi designed the
sacristy, where the pure
geometric forms exude a
sense of space, rhythm and
severity. The nave contains
works by Donatello, Lippi,
Bronzino and Rosso. To the
right, on the way out, there
is a cloister and Michel-
angelo's stately staircase
leading up to the Medici
library (Biblioteca
Laurenziana), an opulent
setting for a fine collection.
Michelangelo also
designed the Medici
funerary chapel (Cappella
dei Principi), where the
stunnings tombs and floor
in *pietra dura* (stones of all
colors cut small and inlaid
like mosaics) make you
wonder where exactly does
architecture stop and
sculpture begin.
★ **Palazzo Medici-**
Riccardi (**C** A4)
→ *Via Cavour, 3*
Tel. 055 276 03 40
Thu-Tue 9am–7pm
The stately palace of

Cosimo the Elder was
commissioned in 1444 from
Michelozzo, his favorite
architect. This Renaissance
gem became a widely
copied model throughout
Italy from the 15th century
onward. It has an inner
courtyard and garden, a
baroque reception room
painted by Giordano and,
above all, a chapel with
Benozzo Gozzoli's
wonderful frescos, at first
glance a *Calvacade of the
Magi*, but teeming with
details about court life.
★ **Cenacolo di Santa**
Apollonia (**C** B3)
→ *Via XXVII Aprile, 1*
Tel. 055 238 86 07
Daily 8.15am–1.50pm

Closed 2nd and 4th M
A sense of dramatic
and Benedictine aus
find striking express
the *Last Supper* (145
by Andrea del Casta
a popular subject fo
monastery refectorie
(*cenacoli*).
★ **Chiostro dello S**
(**C** C3)
→ *Via Cavour, 69*
Tel. 055 238 86 04
Mon, Thu, Sat 8.15am
This Intimist cloister
grisaille (gray monoc
series of frescos pai
Andrea del Sarto (16
century) and his pup
Franciabigio. Taking
from Michelangelo,
imbued these scene

C

Map 5

MUSEO DI
SAN MARCO

GIARDINO
DEI
SEMPLICI

MUSEO
BOTANIC

CHIOSTRO
DELLO SCALZO

CORTE
D'ASSISE
E D'APPELLO

PALAZZO
PANDOLFINI

QUESTURA

OSPEDALE
MILITARE

POR S. GA

Pia della l

Piazza
della
Indipendenza

BARBANO

STROZZI

VIA CAVOUR

VIA G. LA PIRA

VIA P. A. MICHELI

VIA VEI

VIA A

VIA SAN GALLO

VIA SAN GALLO

VIA GINO CAPPONI

VIA G. SALVESTRINA

VIA SAN GALLO

VIA DELLE RUOTE

VIA SAN REPARATA

VIA XXVII APRILE

VIA SAN ZANOBI

VIA SAN GALLO

VIA BONIFACIO LUPI

VIA DUCA D'AOSTA

VIA D. MANTELLATE

VIA SANTA REPARATA

VIA SAN ZANOBI

VIA SANTA CATERINA D'ALESSANDRIA

VIALE SPARTACO LAVAGNINI

VIA S. CATERINA D'ALESSANDRIA

VIA E. POGGI

VIA G. DOLFI

VIA LORENZO X

VIALE GIOVANNI MILTON

VIA A. POLIZIANO

VIA LEONE X

VIA LORENZO X

VIA C. LANDINO

VIALE IL MAGNIFICO

VIA LORENZO IL MAGNIFICO

CHIESA RUSSA
ORTODOSSA

VIALE GIOVANNI MILTON

VIALE GIOVANNI MILTON

VIA XX SETTEMBRE

VIA XX SETTEMBRE

VIA F.LLI RUFFINI

VIA MUGNONE

TORRENTE MUGNONE

VIA XX SETTEMBRE

165 yards

150 m   75   0

PALAZZO MEDICI-RICCARDI

SAN LORENZO

An entire district sprang up as a result of the impetus given by the first Medici, Cosimo Il Vecchio (the Elder), and then by Lorenzo the Magnificent – look for their impressive palace, their library, and the church of San Lorenzo, one of Florence's most precious treasures. Further north is the university district, and the flow of students passing through Piazza San Marco makes it one of the liveliest squares in the city. It is bordered by two major monuments: the convent of San Marco, which boasts some of Fra Angelico's most mystical work, and the Academy of Fine Arts. Many Florentines live in northeast Florence, which is why so many authentic groceries and restaurants are here.

MERCATO CENTRALE   ZÀ-ZÀ

RESTAURANTS

Mercato Centrale (C A4)
→ Piazza di Mercato Centrale. Mon-Sat 7am–2pm (4–7pm Sat, winter)
Surrounded by the leather market, this beautiful 19th-century covered market is a riot of colors, fragrances and flavors. This is the perfect place for lunch: visit Nerbone to see proprietors and laborers enjoying tripe at the same table (5 €); or go to Perini to sample the grocer's crostini and put together a mouthwatering picnic.

Il Vegetariano (C B2)
→ Via delle Ruote, 30r
Tel. 055 47 50 30
Daily 12.30–3pm, 7.30pm–midnight. Closed Sat, Sun lunch and Mon
One of Florence's few vegetarian restaurants, with a shady arbor for eating al fresco in the summer and a cozy interior in the winter. Zucchini and mushroom risotto, eggplant gratin, chocolate cake, crumble, cheesecake. Dishes 6 €.

Zà-Zà (C A4)
→ Piazza di Mercato Centrale, 26 r
Tel. 055 21 54 11
Mon-Sat lunch and dinner
This delightful restaurant is always packed. In summer, diners sit on the terrace overlooking the market. Soups, tagliata al tartufo (minced beef in a truffle sauce on a bed of rocket) and apple puffs. Dishes 10 €.

Lo Skipper (C C4)
→ Via degli Alfani, 78a/r
Tel. 055 28 40 19.
Daily 10am–midnight.
Closed Sat lunch and Sun
This is the sailing club restaurant, tucked away to the right of the Opificio delle Pietre Dure. The Neapolitan chef and owner lovingly prepares Tuscan dishes with an exotic twist. Every month he celebrates the flavors of a particular region or country: Greece, Mexico, Sicily. Booking essential. Dishes 8 –10 €.

Le Tre Panche (C F1)
→ Via A. Pacinotti, 32r
Tel. 055 583 724
Mon-Sat noon–3pm, 8pm–midnight
As its name suggests, this restaurant has just three benches. Delicious wine by the carafe, authentic risotto and pasta dishes. Dishes 10 €.

Perseus (C D1)
→ Viale Don G. Minzoni, 10r. Tel. 055 58 82 26
Mon-Sat noon–2.30pm, 7.30–11pm

ARIANO   CAFFELATTE   ALL'ANCORA SECCA

reat yourself to a succulent cut of meat in typically Florentine ompany. Everything on he menu in this estaurant is exquisite. Dishes 11–13 €.

CAFÉS, PATISSERIES

Caffelatte (C C4)
→ Via degli Alfani, 39r
Tel. 055 24 78 878
Daily 8am–midnight
Closed Sun
The owner, a past master at making coffee, has given this former dairy a new lease of life. Delicious cakes and very good coffee indeed.
Robiglio (C C4)
→ Via dei Servi, 112r
Tel. 055 212 784
Mon-Sun 7.30am–7.30pm
This traditional patisserie has enjoyed an excellent reputation since 1928. Specialty: la torta campagnola, pine seed and almond shortbread and cake made with chestnut flour: delicious.

BARS, WINE BARS, CLUBS

Fratelli Zanobini (C A4)
→ Via Sant'Antonino, 47r
Tel. 055 239 68 50
Daily 8am–2pm, 3.30–8pm.

Closed Sun
A wine cellar stocking the best Chianti (from Vernaccia to Brunello). Glass of wine 1 –5 €.
Caracol (C C4)
→ Via de' Ginori, 10r
Tel. 055 21 14 27
Tue-Sun 5.30pm–1.30am
(2.30am Fri-Sat)
This caliente Mexican bar is buzzing when it's time for an aperitif: aficionados congregate at the counter to sip a marguarita or tequila. Both the music and décor have a distinctly Latin feel. Flamenco on Sun, concerts on Wed.
Rubirosa (C A2)
→ Viale F. Strozzi, 18-20r
Tel. 055 230 28 85
Tue-Sun 8–2am
In front of the monumental Fortezza da Basso (16th century), this sophisticated bar is an up-market meeting place for night owls preparing to hit the town. Beer 4 €.
Club Badu (C B2)
→ Via Zanobi, 114b
Tel. 055 830 35 13
Wed-Sun 10.30pm–4am
Formerly Soulciety, the Florentine soul club, this venue has changed tempo and now plays hip-hop, reggae and funk. It was good fun before, we hope it will still be now.

SHOPPING

All'Ancora Secca (C A4)
→ Via de' Ginori, 21r
Tel. 055 21 64 23
Mon 3–7pm; Tue-Sun
10am–2pm, 3–7pm
Beautifully designed diaries, albums and notebooks bound by Antonella's nimble fingers. Intricately designed clasps, soft leather, warm colors and marbled paper.
La Ménagère (C A4)
→ Via de' Ginori, 8r
Tel. 055 21 38 75
Mon 3.30–7.30pm;
Tue-Sat 9am–1pm, 3.30–7.30pm
This well-established store, founded in 1896, sells ultra-modern household goods: from traditional utensils to the latest in designer appliances; stocks all you need for successful Italian cookery.
Antica Occhialeria (C C1)
→ Via San Gallo, 130r
Tel. 055 47 30 55
Tue-Sat 9.30am–7.30pm
The place for sunglasses, an accessory no self-respecting Italian is seen without. This optician revamps the chic styles of the 1950s–70s with vivid frames. Pair 49 €.

Renato (C C1)
→ Via San Gallo, 199r
Tel. 055 48 35 48
Mon-Sat 9am–6pm
A stylish cut in unique surroundings: two white metal floors, futurist hairdryers and art shows. The staff lavishing attention on customers reputedly work for the best hairdresser in Florence. The price of beauty: 80 €.
Da Fernando (C D1)
→ Via Don Minzoni, 38r
Tel. 055 58 75 40
Mon-Sat 7am–7.30pm
Closed Wed afternoon
Go out of your way for this Ali Baba's cave of fruit, vegetables and wine, some distance from the center. The shelves are stacked with appetizing jars of fruit in syrup, vegetables sotto olio and truffle-flavored olive oil. Finish off the gastronomic odyssey at the Perseus restaurant, a short distance away (see under 'Restaurants').
Solo Donna (C B3)
→ Via San Gallo, 43r
Tel. 055 47 79 18
Tue-Sat 9.30am–1pm,
4-7.30pm. Closed Mon am
Italian shoes for women. Reasonably-priced, given the quality of the leather and the craftsmanship.

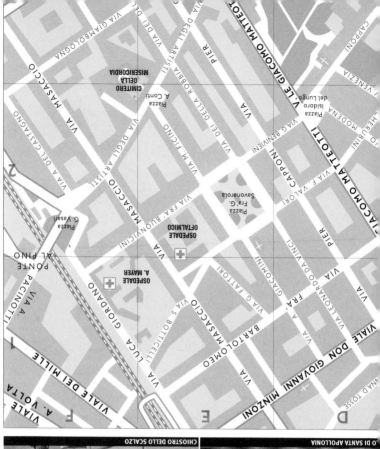

PIAZZA DELLA SANTISSIMA ANNUNZIATA

MUSEO ARCHEOLOGICO

of St John the
with an almost
ral quality.
eo di San Marco

a San Marco
238 86 08
8.30am–1.50pm
t & Sun)
ene monastery
ages the
plation of the work
ngelico. The 15th-
monk and artist
re, decorating each
n frescos full of grace
h, like his angelic
iation.
eria dell'Accademia
emia di Belle Arti)

icasoli, 60

Tel. 055 238 86 09
Tue-Sun 8.15am–6.50pm
(10pm Sat in summer)
In the Academy of Fine Arts
run by Michelangelo, this
collection of sculptures
served as models for
students to copy. Standing
in an immense space are
Michelangelo's audacious
David, realized in his early
period, and his dramatic
Pietà and *Four Prisoners*,
sculpted when he was
more mature and able to
draw raw emotion from the
rough marble.
★ **Spedale degli**
Innocenti (C C4)
→ *Piazza della Santissima*
Annunziata, 12
Tel. 055 249 17 08

Thu-Tue 8.30am–2pm
Brunelleschi's hospital
once cared for abandoned
children, as can be seen
from the roundels realized
by the Della Robbias. It is
now a museum with some
moving Madonnas and
Child and a sensational
Ghirlandaio.
★ **Piazza della**   (**C** C4)
Santissima Annunziata
A typically Renaissance
square by Brunelleschi,
who created a sense of
unity with the slender-
columned porticos. On the
eastern side is the Spedale
degli Innocenti. On the
northern side stands the
church of the Santissima
Annunziata (15th century),

by Michelozzo. This church
was richly decorated in
baroque style, unusual for
Florence, because it
contains a miraculous
painting of the Virgin Mary.
★ **Museo Archeologico**
(**C** C4)
→ *Via della Colonna 38*
Tel. 055 23 575. Mon 2–7pm;
Tue, Thu 8.30am–7pm; Wed,
Fri, Sun, Sat 8.30am–2pm
and Sat 8–11pm in summer
Etruscan collection that
dates back to the 9th
century BC: sarcophagi,
cinerary urns and votive
bronzes. Egypt and Greece
are well represented with
priceless vases showing
the influence of Ancient
Greece on Etruscan art.

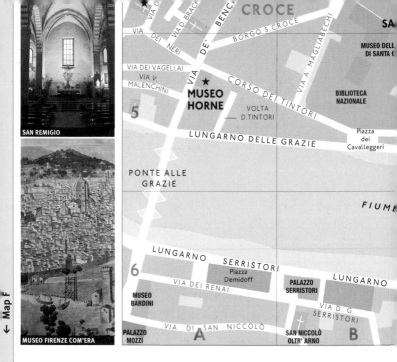

SAN REMIGIO

MUSEO FIRENZE COM'ERA

D

★ Piazza Santa Croce
(**D** B4)

This spacious square has always been used for public meetings: the Franciscans once preached here beside a small oratory dedicated to the holy cross (*santa croce*), the carnival was held here, as were the matches of *calcio*, a type of very rough soccer, dating back to antiquity and still played in June on the square, in medieval costumes. On the northwest side, a plaque shows the level reached by flood waters in 1966.

★ Santa Croce (**D** B4)
→ *Piazza Santa Croce, 16*
Tel. 055 24 46 18
Church: Mon-Sat 8am–

6.30pm (closed between 12.30 and 3pm in Nov-Feb); Sun 8am–1pm, 3–6pm Cappella dei Pazzi & Museo: Thu-Tue 10am–6pm
This lavishly decorated Franciscan church has become Florence's pantheon: many illustrious figures have been buried here (Machiavelli and Michelangelo). The two chapels to the right of the choir contain frescos, masterpieces by the great Giotto (14th century). In the left transept, the *Crucifix* by Donatello displays surprising realism. To the right of the church, the tranquil cloister leads to the museum (*Crucifix* by

Cimabue) and the Pazzi Chapel (1443–78), a Florentine Renaissance wonder by Brunelleschi.

★ Museo Horne (**D** A5)
→ *Via de' Benci, 6*
Tel. 055 24 46 61
Mon-Sat 9am–1pm (and 8.30–11.30pm Mon)
A Renaissance palace, bought and tastefully decorated by 19th-century English architect and art historian H. P. Horne. Wonderful furniture and paintings by Giotto, Beccafumi and Lippi. There are some rare capitals in the courtyard.

★ San Remigio (**D** A4)
→ *Via San Remigio, 4*
Tel. 055 28 47 89

Daily 9–11am, 4–7pm
This church stands i[n] maze of medieval al[leys] An austere and eleg[ant] example of Florentin[e] Gothic, its interior ra[diates] a contemplative atmosphere under t[he] Byzantine gaze of a *Madonna and Child* school of Cimabue (

★ Museo Firenze com'era (**D** A2)
→ *Via dell' Oriuolo, [2]*
Tel. 055 261 65 45
Fri-Wed 9am–2pm
'The Museum of Flo[rence] as it once was'. Fasc[inating] museum charting th[e] urban development [of the] city from Roman tim[es to] the 19th century: ma[ny]

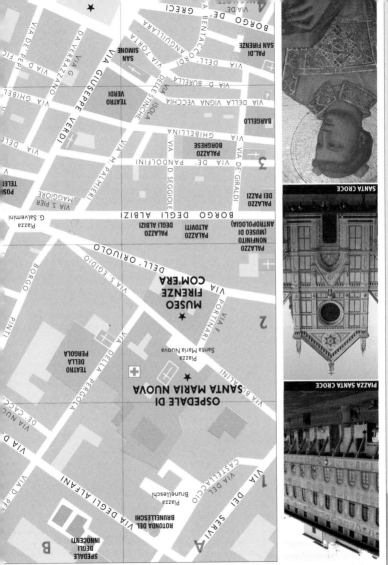

This has been the working-class hub of the city for centuries, owing to the large population of leather workers who still ply their trade around Santa Croce and in the medieval streets to the west. The piazza has always been the focus of festivals, games and entertainment of all kinds. In the evening, theaters, jazz clubs, clubs and bars come to life. This district is ideal for window-shopping and people watching, in the Borgo degli Albizi, with its Renaissance palaces, or the flea, fruit and vegetable markets in the east. For art lovers there is Santa Croce, the largest Franciscan basilica in Italy, as well as smaller churches and museums, no less interesting for being off the beaten track.

OSTERIA DE BENCI   MAGO MERLINO TEA HOUSE

RESTAURANTS

Ramraj (**D** D4)
→ *Via Ghibellina, 61r*
*Tel. 055 24 09 99. Daily
10am–3.30pm, 5.30–11pm*
A taste of exotic spices in the Tuscan capital: the colors and flavors of India by a chef from Bangalore. Take out or enjoy your meal in the square to the sound of music from the subcontinent (when it isn't drowned out by the TV). Menu 8 €.

Pizzaiuolo (**D** D3)
→ *Via de' Macci, 113r*
*Tel. 055 24 11 71
Mon-Sat 12.30–3pm,
7.30pm–12.30am*
The best pizzeria in the city run by Neapolitans who import the mozzarella from their home town. Reservation essential. À la carte 10 €.

Ruth's (**D** C2)
→ *Via L. C. Farini, 2A*
*Tel. 055 248 08 88
Sun-Fri 12.30–2.30pm,
8–10pm*
Next door to the synagogue, an orthodox Kosher restaurant for vegetarians bored with the eternal pasta. Fish couscous, Middle-Eastern platter and strudel.
À la carte 12 €.

Osteria de Benci (**D** A5)
→ *Via de' Benci, 13r*
*Tel. 055 234 49 23
Daily lunch and dinner.
Closed Sun*
This restaurant, opened by a group of friends, has a terrace perfect for warm evenings. Rustic yet sophisticated cuisine: chunky soups, salads and pasta. À la carte 20 €.

La Pentola d'Oro (**D** C2)
→ *Via di Mezzo, 24r*
*Tel. 055 24 18 08
Mon-Sat 7.30–11.30pm*
Follow the lead of the garrulous chef, a patriotic Tuscan with impeccable taste, who has dared to reinvent cuisine by referring back to Etruscan history. Your tastebuds will definitely be in for a shock (we're talking wild boar in chocolate!). An institution. À la carte 30 €.

CAFÉS, ICE CREAM PARLORS

Cibreo (**D** D3)
→ *Via A. D. Verrochio, 5r*
*Tel. 055 248 08 88
Tue-Sat 8am–1am*
Better known for the legendary restaurant and *trattoria* opposite, Cibreo serves coffee in delicate white porcelain cups. The paneled dining room is cozy in winter. Delicious snacks. Coffee 1.50 €.

DELLA PERGOLA | JAZZ CLUB | ARTI E MESTIERI

Vivoli (**D** A3)
→ Via Isola delle Stinche,
7r. Tel. 055 29 23 34
Tue-Sat 8am–1am;
Sun 9.30am–1am
The ice cream parlor
to visit in Florence:
deliciously creamy
gelati that make the
long queue worthwhile.

**Mago Merlino
Tea House** (**D** C2)
→ Via de' Pilastri, 31r
Tel. 055 24 29 70
Daily 5–8pm
Soft music, hookahs,
subdued lighting,
Oriental rugs and quiet
niches: teas from all over
the world, delicious cakes
(5 €)... and, occasionally,
shows in the evening.
Annual (10 €) or weekly
pass (2 €).

BARS, CLUBS,
THEATERS

Rex (**D** B2)
→ Via Fiesolana, 25r
Tel. 055 248 03 31
Daily 5pm–3am
Closed June 15–Sep 15
Lighting effects playing
over mosaics : this bar is
a favorite with laid-back
20-somethings when it's
time for an aperitif (2 €),
always served with a
generous helping of
snacks. Great music in
the evening.

Teatro Verdi (**D** B3)
→ Via Ghibellina; 91r
Tel. 055 21 23 20/239 62 42
Mon-Sat 10am–1pm, 4–7pm
Opera house, founded in
1854, puts on eclectic
programs of classical
music, pop and rock.

Teatro della Pergola
(**D** B2)
→ Via della Pergola, 12/32
Tel. 055 22 641
Mon-Sat 9.30am–1pm,
3.30–6.45pm; Sun 10am–
12.15pm. Concerts Sat-Sun
4pm, 9pm
This gem, designed in
1652 for the Great Duke,
is famous as the oldest
theater in Italy. Donizetti,
Verdi and Bellini once
performed here. Fine
programs of classical
music and drama.

Jazz Club (**D** B2)
→ Via Nuova de' Caccini, 3
Tel. 055 247 97 00
Tue-Sun 9.30pm–1am
Closed June–Aug
Since the 1980s, the club
has acquired a proven
track-record with various
international ensembles.
Special guest on Tue.
Membership card 5 €,
beer 5 €.

Maramao (**D** C3)
→ Via de Macci, 79r
Tel. 055 244 341
Tue-Sat 11pm–3am
Closed May–Sep
This club, with its cool hip

Dolce Vita atmosphere,
is packed all night long:
getting onto the dance
floor is something of a
feat on a Sat evening.
Admission 10 €.

Exmud (**D** A5/B5)
→ Corso dei Tintori, 4
Tel. 055 263 85 83
Thu-Sat 11pm–4.30am
Exceptional house music:
electronic, drum 'n bass,
groove, house and video.
Admission 5 –8 €.

Le Murate (**D** D4)
→ Via dell' Agnolo
Tel. 055 239 90 00.
Wed-Sat at 9pm (May 15–
Sep 15)
Former women's prison,
now an open-air venue
for jazz, movies and other
shows (summer). Off the
wall and very popular.

SHOPPING

Arti e Mestieri (**D** A3)
→ Borgo degli Albizi, 67r
Tel. 055 23 47 440
Tue-Sat 10am–7.30pm;
Mon 2.30–7.30pm
Gift ideas for the home
created by imaginative
Italian designers. Soap
dishes masquerading as
fish-filled lakes, snake
shelves, lip ashtrays...

Artigiano Anny (**D** A3)
→ Borgo degli Albizi, 45r
Tel. 055 234 22 26.
Mon-Sat 10.30am–2pm,

3–7.30pm
Gorgeous jewelry made
of crystal and decorated
with ruby red flower
motifs. Rings or earrings
12–30 €.

A piedi nudi nel parco
(**D** B3)
Borgo degli Albizi, 46r
Tel. 055 234 07 68
Mon-Sat 10am–7.30pm
Closed Mon am in winter,
Sat pm in summer
Alternative fashion
designs by the owner of
the store, and a good
selection of creations by
other contemporary
Italian stylists.

Sbigoli (**D** B3)
→ Via San Egidio, 4r
Tel. 055 24 79 713
Mon-Sat 9am–1pm, 3.30–
7.30pm. Closed Mon am in
winter, Sat pm in summer
Crockery inspired by
Renaissance majolica
and Umbrian or Tuscan
faïence. Dishes, vases
and lamps, mainly made
at the rear of the store.
Affordable prices.

Il Ponte (**D** C2)
→ Via di Mezzo, 42b
Tel. 055 24 06 17
Tue-Sat 4–7.30pm
A politically committed,
modern art gallery. The
son of a printer, Andrea
Alibrandi, publishes
some superb catalogues
himself.

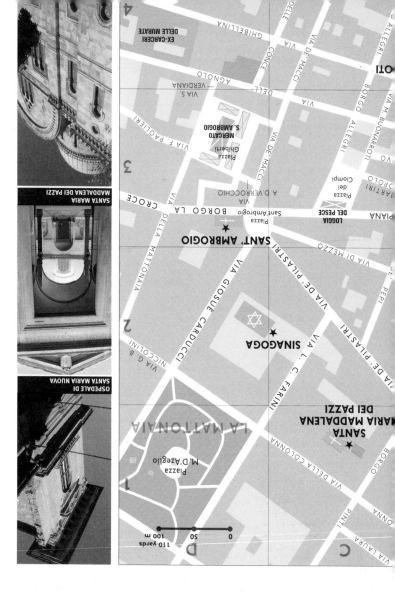

VIA PIETRO THOUAR

VIA GIUSEPPE

VIA DEI MALCONTENTI 5

VIA DELLE CASINE

VIA TRIPOLI

Piazza Piave

LUNGARNO DELLA ZECCA VECCHIA

TORRE DELLA ZECCA

NO

PESCAIA DI SAN NICCOLÒ 6

Piazza Giuseppe Poggi

PORTA S. NICCOLÒ

LUNGARNO B. CELLINI

C D

SANT'AMBROGIO

CASA BUONARROTI

Map F →

and paintings, ng a remarkable ce of the Medici v Justus Van Utens entury).
edale di Santa Nuova (D A2)
ᴢa Santa Maria Nuova ᴘressive portico ᴇd by Buontalenti in century adorns the açade of the l (still operational), ᴅ in the 13th century ᴘ Portinari, the f Dante's beloved . The baroque of Sant'Egidio at its center.
aria Maddalena ᴢi (D C1)
ᴏ Pinti, 58

Tel. 055 247 84 20
Daily 9am–noon (10.45am Sun), 5–5.20pm and 6.10–7pm (mass at 5.30pm)
Once through the cloister by Giuliano da Sangallo (late 15th century) and the church with its 17th-century decoration, you enter a hidden labyrinth leading to the Chapter House: this has a *Crucifixion* (1495) by Perugino, which is admirable for its restraint and tenderness.
★ **Sinagoga (D** D2)
→ Via L. C. Farini, 4
Tel. 055 24 52
Sun-Thu 10am–5pm in April-May and Sep-Oct; until 3pm Nov-March; until 6pm in June-Aug; Fri 10am–1.30pm

This 19th-century building is a marvel of oriental splendor: Byzantine outside, Moorish inside. Florence's synagogue replaced those of the Jewish ghetto that had been situated on the site of the Piazza della Repubblica since the 16th century.
★ **Sant' Ambrogio (D** D3)
→ Piazza Sant' Ambrogio
Tel. 055 24 01 04. Daily 7.30am–noon, 4.15–7pm
Close by some colorful markets, this 13th-century church (dating back to the 5th) became a eucharistic shrine following a miracle in 1230: it contains an exquisite tabernacle by Mino da Fiesole (1483) to

house the chalice in which the wine was transformed into blood. There are a number of fine frescos and *sinopias* (drafts).
★ **Casa Buonarroti (D** C3)
→ Via Ghibellina, 70
Tel. 055 24 17 52
Wed-Mon 9.30am–2pm
Michelangelo's memory is preserved in this house, bought before he left for Rome. Superb youthful works, such as the bas-reliefs realized by the 16-year-old genius, who introduced a sense of movement and doubt into the art of the end of the Renaissance: the *Battle of the Centaurs*, the *Madonna della Scala* and a *Crucifix*.

VIA MAGGIO   **SANTO SPIRITO**   **CAPPELLA BRANCACCI**

★ **Palazzo Pitti (E** E3)
→ *Piazza de' Pitti*
Tel. 055 238 86 14
Galleria Palatina,
Appartamenti Monumentali:
Tue–Sun 8.30am–6.50pm
(9pm Tue–Fri, 10pm Sat, 8pm
Sun June 15–Sep 15).
Gallerie d'Arte Moderna,
del Costume, Museo degli
Argenti: Tue–Sun 8.15am–2pm
Closed 2nd, 4th Sun and 1st,
3rd, 5th Mon
The grandest of Renaissance
buildings, Palazzo Pitti was
built to plans by Brunelle-
schi that had been rejected
by Cosimo the Elder and
bought by one of his rivals,
the banker Pitti, in 1457.
Later Medici rulers decided
to live there, hence the

luxurious apartments. The
north wing contains the
magnificent collection of the
Palatine Gallery: 25 rooms
packed with Italian paintings
that once belonged to the
grand dukes of Tuscany:
Raphael, Titian and Andrea
del Sarto... An unmissable
complement to the Uffizi's
collections. On the same
floor is the Costume Gallery
and, on the second floor, the
Gallery of Modern Art
(Italian painting from the
late 1700s to the early
1900s). On the ground floor
is the Museo degli Argenti:
a dramatic setting for a
collection of vases, jewelry
and *pietra dura* (hard
stone) mosaics.

★ **Giardino di Boboli (E** E3)
→ *Piazza de' Pitti/Porta*
Romana. Tel. 055 29 48 83
Daily 8.15am–7.30pm
(4.30pm winter)
Formal, Italian-style garden
(16th–17th century). The
natural hills and dales of
the gardens are dotted
randomly with a sculpted
grotto, fountains, statues,
cypress trees and groves.
Stunning views of Florence
and the hills from the
Porcelain Museum, above
the Neptune Fountain and
the Amphitheater.

★ **Museo Zoologico
della Specola (E** D3)
→ *Via Romana 17*
Tel. 055 228 82 51
Thu–Tue 9am–1pm

Designed in the 17t..
century for educatic
purposes, this colle
of anatomical waxw
incredibly realistic a
largest in the world
not for the squeam
would do better to
concentrate on the
zoological collectio
★ **San Felice (E** D
→ *Piazza San Felice*
Tel. 055 22 17 06
Daily 9am–noon, 4–
This unusual, auste
century façade con
some fascinating pa
a *Crucifix* by the sch
Giotto and a *Mador*
Ghirlandaio.
★ **Via Maggio (E** E
This road stretches

E

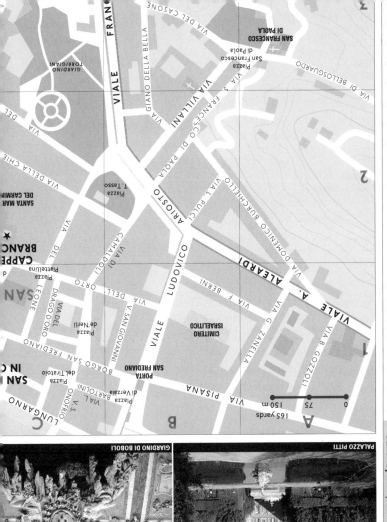

Santo Spirito / San Frediano

The Oltrarno, or left bank, which was belatedly brought within the ramparts in the 13th century, is more provincial in atmosphere. Although the stately Palazzo Pitti extends the Medici city, the districts of Santo Spirito and San Frediano are still the home of antique dealers and artisans. By day, workshops ring to the sound of tools that once built the beautiful monuments adorning the streets of Florence. The Boboli Garden (Giardino di Boboli) is an impressive example of a Tuscan-style landscaped sculpture gardens. In the evenings, smartly dressed Florentines socialize on the squares and in the restaurants and bars.

OSTERIA SANTO SPIRITO · RICCHI

RESTAURANTS

Da Pruto (**E** C2)
→ *Piazza T. Tasso, 9r*
Tel. 055 22 22 19
*Daily lunch and dinner
Closed Mon*
Somewhat off the beaten track on a pretty square surrounding a small sport's ground. The atmosphere is cheap and cheerful at lunchtime, and more traditional in the evening. Tasty fish specialties: *tagliatelle all'astice* (lobster). Weekday lunch menu 6–8 €.

Cambi (**E** C1)
→ *Via San Onofrio, 1r*
Tel. 055 21 71 34
Mon-Sat 12.30–2.30pm, 7.30–10.30pm
Tourists and local residents squeeze into this beautiful vaulted dining room plastered with old photos to savor *lardo di collonata* and *trippe alla fiorentina*. Those on a diet shouldn't come here. Terrace in the summer. Booking essential. À la carte 16 €.

Osteria Santo Spirito (**E** D2)
→ *Piazza Santo Spirito, 16r*
Tel. 055 238 23 83. *Daily 12.15–3pm, 7.45–11pm*
Multicolored interior, terrace overlooking the delightful Santo Spirito square and a style of cuisine that reinvents traditional Tuscan flavors. This restaurant has a youthful, lively feel – perfect for enjoying a glass or more of excellent wine. À la carte 20 €.

Trattoria Angiolino (**E** D1)
→ *Via Santo Spirito, 36r*
Tel. 055 239 89 76
*Daily lunch and dinner
Closed Mon*
The floorshow in this restaurant is provided by the kitchens: adorned with old cauldrons and garlands of tomatoes, garlic and corn, this splendid scene can be seen from the dining room. Stylish service and traditional dishes: the delicious rib of beef with *patate all'arrosto* (roast potatoes) is the best in the city. À la carte 20 €.

Trattoria del Carmine (**E** C1)
→ *Piazza del Carmine, 18r*
Tel. 055 21 86 01. *Mon-Sat noon–3pm, 7pm– midnight*
A classy place for an exquisite meal: rabbit with olives, salted cod cooked Livorno style and very good desserts. Excellent Chiantis. Book ahead. À la carte 20 €.

I Quattro Leoni (**E** E2)
→ *Via de' Vellutini, 1r*
Tel. 055 21 85 62

PITTI · DOLCE VITA · ANTICO SETIFICIO FIORENTINO

Daily noon–2.30pm,
7.30–11pm
Plentiful Tuscan cuisine in a rustic-style dining room: excellent meat and seasonal dishes. The terrace overlooking a quiet square is very popular. Booking essential. À la carte 25 €.

CAFÉS, ICE CREAM PARLORS

Ricchi (E D2)
→ Piazza Santo Spirito, 8/9r. Tel. 055 21 58 64
Daily 7–1am (9pm winter)
The place to go for cakes, ice creams or a pre-dinner aperitif that can be sipped on the terrace or in the intimate dining room where you can admire the extraordinary plans designed by artists for the façade of Santo Spirito in 1981.
Caffè Pitti (E E2)
→ Piazza de' Pitti, 9
Tel. 055 239 98 63
Daily 9am–1am
A maze of little rooms and plush sofas. Curl up and savor a prosecco (sparkling white wine).
Caffè Artegiani (E E2)
→ Via dello Sprone, 16r
Tel. 055 29 18 82
Mon-Sat 9am–11pm
For those craving some peace and quiet, this

small two-floor café between the Pitti Palace and the Via Maggio is an ideal stop off; there you can read, write, and enjoy a well-earned rest. Coffee and snacks.

BARS, CLUBS

Dolce Vita (E C1)
→ Piazza del Carmine
Tel. 055 28 45 95
Daily 5.30pm–1.30am
(2am Fri and Sat)
One of the first trendy bars in Florence. It still sets the trend.
Cabiria (E D2)
→ Piazza Santo Spirito, 4r
Tel. 055 215 732
Daily 8am–1am (2am Fri-Sun). Closed Tue in winter
A must for night owls who enjoy the music's soft beat. Stand between the wall and the bar or relax in the seating area.
Universale (E A1)
→ Via Pisana, 77r
Tel. 055 22 11 22
Wed-Sun 7pm–3am
Former movie theater, converted into a massive versatile venue: eat, drink, dance or watch concerts and shows.
Sotto Sopra (E D2)
→ Via Serragli, 48r
Tel. 055 28 23 40
Mon-Sat 6.30pm–2am
One of the best clubs to

visit in the area. Latin beats, house and drum 'n bass in the vaulted cellar. Free admission.

SHOPPING

**Francesco da Firenze
(E** D1)
→ Via Santo Spirito, 62r
Tel. 055 21 24 28
Mon-Sat 9am–1pm,
3–7.30pm (8pm summer)
Don't be deterred by the badly lit window: the shoes for men and women, handmade by Francesco in the rear of the store, are fabulous. Elegant and perennially fashionable.
Angela Caputi (E E2)
→ Borgo San Jacopo, 82r
Tel. 055 21 29 72
Tue-Sat 10am–1pm, 3.30–7.30pm; Mon 3.30-7.30pm
Monochrome resin jewelry that sparkles like glass: gorgeous braids and flowers.
**Cristina e suoi colori
(E** D1)
→ Borgo San Frediano, 53r
Tel. 055 26 86 05
Tue-Sat 10am–1pm, 3.30-7.30pm; Mon 3.30-7.30pm
A lovely jumble of bags, scarves and hats: felt or wool for winter, straw and cotton in summer. Cristina designs and knits the fabrics herself.

**Antico Setificio
Fiorentino (E** C1)
→ Via L. Bartolini, 4
Tel. 055 21 38 61
Mon-Fri 9am–1pm, 2–5pm
A magical store where the Florentine art of silk-making is still very much alive: Renaissance damasks, brocades and taffetas are woven on 18th-century looms.
Michala Milwertz (E C1)
→ Borgo San Frediano, 159r. Tel. 055 22 96 52
Tue-Sat 10am–1pm, 3.30-7.30pm; Mon 3.30-7.30pm
A colorful store full of surprises. The vivid colors of Italy combined with the stylish forms of Denmark.
Scaparra Filadelfio (E C2)
→ Via del Leone, 35r
Tel. 055 28 00 56. Mon-Fri 8am–noon, 2–6.30pm
Wrought iron in all its glory: chandeliers, wall lamps, bed frames, all intricately worked. Adjacent studio.
Valerio Romanelli (E C2)
→ Via del Leone, 43r
Tel. 055 29 04 86
Mon-Fri 8.30am–12.30pm, 2–7.30pm; Sat 8.30am-12.30pm
Another store-cum-studio devoted to the local tradition of gilded wood: trays, frames, boxes. From luxury goods to reasonably-priced items.

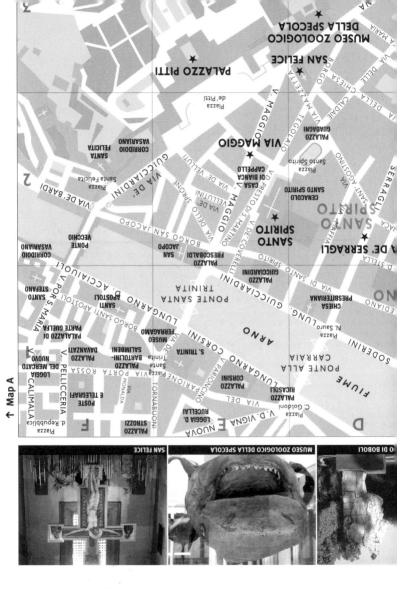

SAN FELICE

MUSEO ZOOLOGICO DELLA SPECOLA

O DI BOBOLI

MUSEO ZOOLOGICO DELLA SPECOLA

★

PALAZZO PITTI

★

SAN FELICE

BORGO

VIA MAZZETTA

DELLE

CALDAIE

A MARIA

Piazza
de' Pitti

VIA MAGGIO

TEGOLAIO

PALAZZO
GUADAGNI

**CORRIDOIO
VASARIANO**

**SANTA
FELICITA**

Piazza
Santo Spirito

VIA MAGGIO

Piazza
Santa Felicita

VIA DE' VELLUTI

CASA DI BIANCA
CAPPELLO

VIA DELLO SPRONE

V. DE' PRESTO D.S. MARTINO

VIA DE' VELLUTINI

**CENACOLO
SANTO SPIRITO**

VIA SANT'AGOSTINO

**SANTO
SPIRITO**

★

VIA DE' BARDI

GUICCIARDINI

BORGO SAN JACOPO

**CORRIDOIO
VASARIANO**

**PONTE
VECCHIO**

SAN
JACOPO

**PALAZZO
FRESCOBALDI**

VIA DI SANTO SPIRITO

SERRAGLIO

D. STELLA

MAFFIA

SDRUCCIOLO

**SANTO
SPIRITO**

★

VIA DE' SERRAGLI

ON

EDIANO

**CHIESA
PRESBITERIANA**

V. PORS. MARIA

**SANTO
STEFANO**

BORGO SANTI APOSTOLI

**SANTI
APOSTOLI**

V. DE' GUICCIARDINI

**PALAZZO
GUICCIARDINI**

LUNGARNO ACCIAIOLI

**PONTE SANTA
TRINITA**

LUNGARNO GUICCIARDINI

N. Sauro

Piazza

LUNGARNO

SODERINI

FIUME

ARNO

**PALAZZO DI
PARTE GUELFA**

**MUSEO
SALVATORE
FERRAGAMO**

S. TRINITA

LUNGARNO CORSINI

Piazza
Santa
Trinita

V. PARIONE

LOGGIA
CALIMALA

Piazza
d. Repubblica

**POSTE
E TELEGRAFI**

**MERCATO
NUOVO**

**PALAZZO
BARTOLINI-
SALIMBENI**

**PALAZZO
DAVANZATI**

VIA PORTA ROSSA

VIA
MONALDA

TORNABUONI

VIA PARIONCINO

V.D. VIGNA NUOVA

**LOGGIA D.
RUCELLAI**

**PALAZZO
STROZZI**

**PALAZZO
CORSINI**

**PALAZZO
RICASOLI**

Piazza
C. Goldoni

VIA DEL
PARIONE

**PONTE ALLA
CARRAIA**

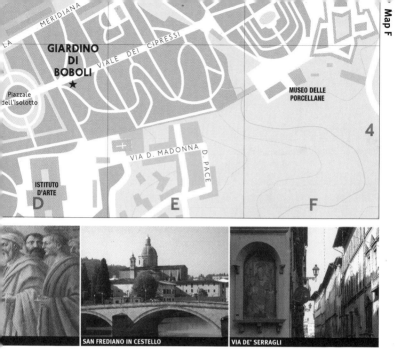

MERIDIANA

LA

VIALE DEI CIPRESSI

**GIARDINO
DI
BOBOLI** ★

Piazzale
dell'Isolotto

**MUSEO DELLE
PORCELLANE**

4

VIA D. MADONNA D. PACE

**ISTITUTO
D'ARTE**

D   **E**   **F**

SAN FREDIANO IN CESTELLO

VIA DE' SERRAGLI

San Felice to the
Trinità bridge, and is
d with statues of the
asons (16th century).
nsion of the Via
Joni, it has some
c palaces (nᵒˢ 30,
13, 11, 7). The finest
at nᵒ 26, decorated
raffito, was built by
lenti in the 16th
for Bianca Cappello,
esan and artists'
who became the
Francesco de Medici.
to Spirito (E E2)
*a Santo Spirito
230 28 85
m–noon, 4–6pm
o:Tue-Sun 9am–2pm
ed square with
cafés and

restaurants. The Palazzo
Guadagni and its great
loggia (16th century) on the
southeast side is worth a
look. The 18th-century
façade of the church forms
a striking contrast with the
interior, which is pure
Brunelleschi. Sangallo
drew his inspiration from
the great master for the
highly successful sacristy
(*Cristo* by Michelangelo).
The nave contains a
Filippino Lippi, from 1504,
while the refectory (to the
left of the façade) boasts a
Crucifixion and a *Last
Supper* by Orcagna (1360).
★ **Cappella Brancacci
(E** C2)
→ *Piazza del Carmine, 14*

*Tel. 055 238 21 95
Wed-Mon 10am–5pm; Sun
and public hols 1–5pm*
To the right of the church of
Santa Maria del Carmine,
and at the end of the
cloister, stands the
fabulous Brancacci Chapel.
The gracious style of
frescos by Masolino and
Lippi is in stark contrast to
the work of Masaccio,
which is remarkable for
its mastery of realism and
the laws of perspective.
★ **San Frediano (E** C1)
→ *Piazza di Cestello, 4
Tel. 055 21 58 16
Daily 9–11.30am, 4.30–
5.30pm (4–5pm summer);
Sun 10–11am, 5–6pm*
This church is entirely

baroque, except for a
Madonna with an
extremely expressive smile
by the school of Pisano
(13th century, third chapel
on the left).
★ **Via de' Serragli (E** D2)
A street full of elegant
palaces: nᵒˢ 8, 9, 17. At the
corner of the Via Santa
Monica, there is a
tabernacle by Bicci (1427).
At nᵒ 144 there is the
Torrigiani Garden. The
street runs into the Piazza
della Calza, where there is
a convent converted into a
hotel which boasts a *Last
Supper* by Franciabigio
(16th century). The Porta
Romana was the way out of
the city in 1326.

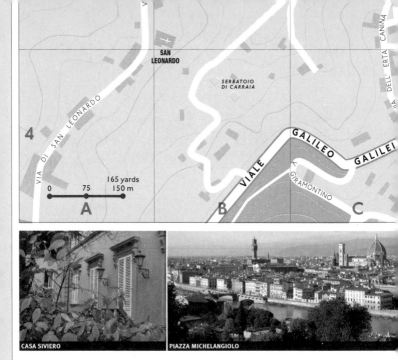

CASA SIVIERO

PIAZZA MICHELANGIOLO

★ **Ponte Vecchio** (**F** A1)
This bridge, constructed on
sturdy pillars, is the only
bridge in Florence to have
withstood wars and floods
since 1345. In the 15th
century it was home to a
foul-smelling market and
was mainly occupied by
hog-butchers who would
dispose of their waste in
the Arno River. In the 16th
century, for reasons of
hygiene, the Grand Duke
removed the butchers and
replaced them with
goldsmiths. They're still
here and today the bridge
acts as a magnet for a
continual stream of
window-shopping tourists.
The Corridor (*Corridoio*

Vasariano, see **A** ★)
running above the stores
was built by Vasari and
allowed the Grand Duke
to avoid the crowds. There
are marvelous views of the
Arno and the city from the
center of the bridge.
★ **Santa Felicità** (**F** A1)
→ *Piazza Santa Felicità*
Tel. 055 21 30 18
Daily 9am–noon, 3–6pm;
Sun 9am–1pm
The façade of the church
on the square is linked to
Vasari's Corridor: the
Medici rulers could watch
services from the inner box.
Living in the Pitti Palace
since the late 16th century,
this became their court
church. Inside, the Capponi

Chapel (first on the right)
was built by Brunelleschi
in 1410, and decorated by
the Mannerist painter
Pontormo in 1525–28 (his
Deposition from the Cross
is magnificent).
★ **Via de' Bardi** (**F** B1)
This is a narrow, little-
known street, where few
walkers stroll in the
shadow of the tall, austere
palaces, brightened by
private gardens. N°s 36 and
28-30, with their inner
courtyards and projecting
cornices, are characteristic
of the 14th and 15th
centuries. On one side, the
church of Santa Lucia dei
Magnoli (mass 5.30–6pm)
contains a *St Lucy* painted

by the Sienese artist
Lorenzetti (14th centu
and an *Annunciation*
one of Botticelli's stu
Don't miss the Mozzi
Palace, a typical 13th
century fortress oppo
the Bardini Museum.
★ **Museo Bardini** (**I**
→ *Piazza de' Mozzi, 1*
Tel. 055 234 24 27
Closed for restoration
This church was conv
into a palace in 1881
Florentine antique de
Stefano Bardini. It no
displays on four floor
eclectic collection an
by Bardini: various o
d'art from the Middle
to the baroque era, n
instruments, fine

F

Beyond the Ponte Vecchio, in the eastern reaches of Florence, visitors can enjoy a quiet stroll with the city on one side and the countryside on the other. Within the city walls, the streets are home to silversmiths, book-binders, engravers and other craftsmen. They are so peaceful it is hard to believe this is one of the hot spots for Florentine nightlife with some excellent restaurants and bars. Outside the ramparts, the legendary layout of the Renaissance city can be clearly seen: Piazzale Michelangiolo, San Miniato and the Forte di Belvedere are best visited on foot to make the most of the stunning panoramic vistas.

I TAROCHI   VOLPE E L'UVA

RESTAURANTS

Bordino (F A1)
→ Via Stracciatella, 9r (before the Costa di S. Giorgio). Tel. 055 21 30 48
Mon-Sat noon–2.30pm, 7.30–10.30pm
You'll get here a good meal at an excellent price: lunch menu 6 €.

I Tarochi (F C2)
→ Via dei Renai, 12/14
Tel. 055 234 39 12. Tue-Sun 12.30–2.30pm, 7pm–1am
Pizzas cooked in a wood-fired oven for a tasty snack in a vaulted dining room. Pizza 6 €.

Antica Mescita (F C2)
→ Via di San Niccolò, 60r
Tel. 055 234 28 36
Mon-Sat noon–3.30pm, 7pm–midnight
Delightful eatery in the crypt of the church of San Niccolò. Dishes 6–8 €.

Enoteca Fuori Porta (F C2)
→ Via del Monte alle Croci, 10r. Tel. 055 23 42 483
Mon-Sat 12.30–3.15pm, 7.15pm–12.15am
Halfway up the San Miniato hillside stands this wine store, popular for its cellar and its *crostini* which sport around ten different cheeses with an array of toppings (*caprino, tartufo, prosciutto*). Views over the ramparts. Dishes 8 €.

Volpe e l'Uva (F A1)
→ Piazza de' Rossi, 1r (after the Piazza Santa Felicità)
Tel. 055 239 81 32
Mon-Sat 10am–8pm
This wine bar is run by a true connoisseur, perfect for lovers of fine wine. It also serves the best Tuscan and French cheeses, as well as delicious cooked meats. Main dish + glass of wine 10–15 €.

Pane & Vino (F C2)
→ Via San Niccolò, 60/70r
Tel. 055 247 69 56
Mon-Sat 8pm–1am
Elegant, delicious Italian nouvelle cuisine, perfectly complemented by a good wine list. One of the best restaurants in the city. Dishes 13 €.

CAFÉS, ICE CREAM PARLORS

Frilli (F C2)
→ Via San Miniato, 5r
Tel. 055 234 50 14
Thu-Tue 3–8pm (midnight in summer)
Tiny ice cream parlor that has been handed down from father to son since 1939. The ice creams are deliciously light.

La Loggia (F D3)
→ Piazzale Michelangiolo, 1
Tel. 055 234 28 32

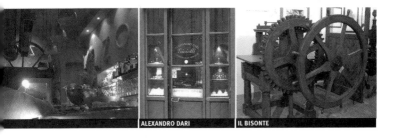

ALEXANDRO DARI   IL BISONTE

Behind the Piazzale, this opulent café–restaurant in a neoclassical loggia affords a fantastic view over the city. Ideal for coffee (the meals are a little pricey).

BARS, CLUBS

James Joyce (F F2)
→ *Lungarno B. Cellini, 1r*
Tel. 055 658 08 56
At the end of the embankment, this real Irish pub with its large tree-lined terrace is very popular on sunny days. Beer 3.50 €.

Rifrullo (F C2)
→ *Via San Niccolo, 55r*
Tel. 055 234 26 21
Daily 8–1am
Open fire in the winter, terrace in the summer and, throughout the year, a long counter made of dark wood covered with snacks for a pre-dinner aperitif. Popular early-evening meeting place for clubbers.

Joe (F C2)
→ *Via dei Renai, 13r*
Tel. 055 24 31 11
Daily 9.30–2am
On the Piazza Demidoff, cocktails flow freely in front of a dazzling range of aperitifs. There isn't usually enough space within the red walls to

accommodate the crowds, which spill out onto the terrace.

Montecarla (F B2)
→ *Via de' Bardi 62r*
Tel. 055 23 40 259
Daily 9pm–4am (5am Fri and Sat)
It is virtually impossible to get into one of the most exuberant bars in the city on a Sat evening: two floors of floral patterns and leopard-print sofas. People come here to curl up and illustrate or color the notebooks on the table. Hefty gin and tonics. Admission and one drink 7.50 €.

Il Jaragua (F C2)
→ *Via dell'erta Canina, 12r*
Tel. 055 234 36 00
Daily 9.30pm–3am
This is *the* Latin club in Florence: give yourself over to the heady rhythms of the merengue, chachacha and salsa after a free lesson provided by the club. Free admission.

Caffè la Torre (F E2)
→ *Lungarno B. Cellini, 65r*
Tel. 055 68 06 43
Daily 11–3am
A popular mecca of Florentine nightlife: for the price of a beer, help yourself to the copious, all-you-can-eat buffet from 7–9pm and take it

out onto the sociable terrace. Evening concerts in the dining room.

SHOPPING

Il Torchio (F B1)
→ *Via de' Bardi 17r*
Tel. 055 234 28 62
Mon-Fri 9am–7.30pm;
Sat 9.30am–1pm
Once inside, just walk past the shelves to watch the craftsmen painstakingly working with magnificent leather. There is a wide selection of diaries, notebooks, albums and frames. Very reasonable prices.

Lisa Corti (F B2)
→ *Via de' Bardi, 58*
Tel. 055 264 56 00
Mon-Sat 10am–1pm, 3.30-7.30pm. Closed Mon am
This vibrant store is a riot of Indian colors. Lisa Corti covers a wide variety of household objects in gorgeous fabrics, bringing Indian sophistication into everyday life.

Alexandro Dari (F C2)
→ *Via di San Niccolò, 115r*
Tel. 055 24 47 47
Mon-Sat 9.30am–1.30pm,
4–7.30pm.
Closed Mon am (winter) &
Sat pm (summer)
A jeweler in a class of his own, a world apart from the Ponte Vecchio where

you can find the best and the worst. In this store extraordinary creativity goes hand in hand with passion and culture: inspiration for the rings is drawn from Gothic architecture, castles, alchemy, music, etc.

Il Bisonte (F D2)
→ *Via di San Niccolò, 24r*
Tel. 055 230 28 85
Mon-Sat 9am–1pm, 3–7pm
A gallery of ancient and modern prints. The name is derived from a work given by Henry Moore to the woman who runs this gallery, Maria Luigia Guaita. There is also a renowned school of engraving at this address.

City Lights Italia (F D2)
→ *Via di San Niccolò, 23r*
Tel. 055 234 78 82. Mon-Fri
10am–1pm, 2–7.30pm
A bookstore-publishing house where you can read poetry published both in its original language and in Dante's Italian. It holds a poetry festival in July as well as special events in the evening.

Certini (F D2)
→ *Via di San Niccolò, 2n*
Tel. 055 23 42 694. Mon-Fri
8.30am–12.30pm, 2.30–7pm
Wrought-iron store and studio: objects with finely chased ivy leaves. From subtle to kitsch.

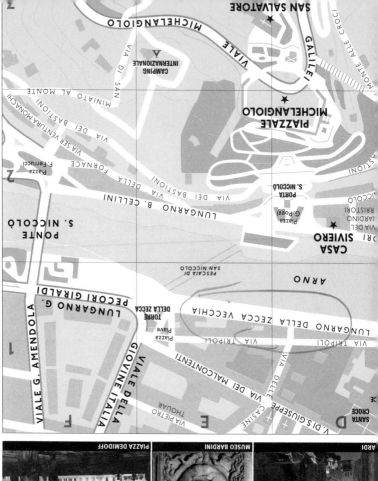

D

E

F

SAN MINIATO AL MONTE ★

CIMITERO DELLE PORTE SANTE

VIALE GA

SAN MINIATO AL

VIA GIRAMONTE

VIALE MICHELANGIOLO

VIA GIRAMONTE

VIALE MICHELANGIOLO

4

...ATORE AL MONTE

SAN MINIATO AL MONTE

FORTE DI BELVEDERE

...tural elements
...sterpieces painted
...pted by Camaino,
...lo and Tiepolo.

...za Demidoff (F C2)
...nt square, named
...hilanthropic
...prince, whose
...ands in the middle
...e garden, where
...take time out in
...le of the trees to
...e view over the
...e National Library
...ta Croce.

...Siviero (F D2)
...rno Serristori, 1-3
...234 52 19
...am–12.30pm;
...–6.30pm
...the secret agent
...historian who

helped restore the Italian
heritage confiscated by the
Nazis. Statues, paintings
and furniture.

★ **Piazzale Michelangiolo (F** D2)
→ Take bus 13 or 12
Like the copy of *David*
oresiding in the square
dedicated to Michelangelo,
it is impossible to tire of
this view: the winding Arno
and, here and there, towers,
domes and campaniles
against the skyline. In the
distance are the mountain-
tops of Fiesole and the
Apennines.

★ **San Salvatore al Monte (F** E3)
→ Via San Salvatore al
Monte, 9

Tel. 055 234 26 40
Daily 8am–noon, 3–6pm
A peaceful stopping place
before San Miniato. Michelangelo, who was very fond
of the understated two-floor
structure built by Il Cronaca
(1504), nicknamed it 'his
pretty country lass'.

★ **San Miniato (F** D3-4)
→ Via del Monte alle Croci, 34
Tel. 055 234 27 31
Daily summer: 8am–7.30pm
(mass 6pm); winter: 8am–
12.30pm, 2.30–7.30pm
There is a memorable view
from the square in front of
the church: on one side, the
idyllic vista of countryside
and city, and on the other,
the serpentine and marble
façade in pure Tuscan

Romanesque style. From its
delicate marble floor with
symbols of animals and
signs of the zodiac, to
Michelozzo's *Cappella del
Crucifisso* (15th century),
the interior radiates
spirituality. Look out
particularly for Spinello
Aretino's fine frescos in the
sacristy (14th century).

★ **Forte di Belvedere (F** A2)
→ Via di San Leonardo
Closed for restoration
A 16th-century bastion:
take a stroll along the Via
del Belvedere and the Via
San Giorgio della Costa
(Galileo's house at n° 27),
with wonderful views:
a true taste of Tuscany.

TRAINS

The best way to get straight into the city center, or to visit the large Tuscan villages, which surround the city.

From London Waterloo
17 hrs by Eurostar (changing in Paris; 8 ½ hrs from Paris-Bercy)

Eurostar
→ Tel. 08705 186 186
Rail Europe Travel Center
→ Tel. 08705 848 848

Stazione Santa Maria Novella
Information
→ www.trenitalia.it
Tel. 8488 88088
Daily 7am–9pm
Reservations and tickets
→ Tel. 055 265 46 18

STAZIONE SANTA MARIA NOVELLA

ATAF CITY BUSES

ORANGE CITY BUSES

Numbered buses are run by the ATAF company in the city and suburbs. Lettered buses in the city center are eco-friendly (electric) and smaller.

Information
→ Bus station, Piazza Adua
Tel. 800 424 500
Detailed map available from the ATAF bus station east of the railroad station

Tickets
On sale from the ATAF bus station, newspaper stands, tobacconists and bars. Tickets are valid for the whole network for a variable period.
1 hr: 1 €
3 hrs: 1.80 €
24 hrs: 4.15 €
2 days: 5.70 €
3 days: 7.25 €
7 days: 12.15 €

Timetable
Eco-friendly buses
→ 8am–8pm
Standard buses
→ 5 or 6am–12.20am
Night buses
→ N° 70 (SMN to Campo di Marte)

Disabled Access
N°s 7, 12, 13, 23, 27, 30 and D have lower platforms and wheelchair space.

BLUE BUSES

Serves the surrounding area; ideal for traveling to small villages. Less expensive than the train.
SITA (**B** D2)
→ Via Santa Catarina da Siena, 17
Tel. 055 2147 21/800 3737
Daily 6am–8.30pm
For San Gimignano, Siena, Volterra, Arezzo

Albergo Scoti (**B** F4)
→ Via Tornabuoni, 7
Tel. 055 239 65 05
This hotel is on the top floor of an old residence in Florence's aristocratic street. No breakfast or private bathroom but large, quiet rooms with a view over the rooftops. Friendly reception and competitive prices. 65 €.

Dali (**D** A2)
→ Via dell'Oriuolo, 17
Tel. 055 234 07 06
A bargain, just behind the Duomo, with large wood-paneled rooms, some of which overlook the magnolia tree in the courtyard. Attentive staff. Free parking (unusual in Florence). No breakfast.
50–65 €.

Orchidea (**D** A3)
→ Borgo degli Albizi, 11
Tel. 055 24 80 346
One of the many palaces on this street. Seven simple rooms without private

bathroom or breakfast, but with relaxing views of wisteria, garden, terrace or street. Informal family atmosphere. 65 €.

Albergo Losanna (**C** E4)
→ Via V. Alfieri, 9
Tel. 055 245 840
Just out of the center to the east in a residential district, this hotel has eight rooms overlooking a courtyard. Breakfast included. Good value for money. 50–70 €.

Mirella (**C** C4)
→ Via degli Alfani, 36
Tel. 055 247 81 70
Ten decent, functional rooms. Enjoy the student quarter without having to put up with the noise. No breakfast. 50–65 €.

77–103 €

Soggiorno Bavaria (**D** A3)
→ Borgo degli Albizi, 26
Tel. 055 234 03 13
This hotel, above the Pandolfi auction house in

the superb 16th-century Montalvo-Ramirez palace designed by Vasari, has 17 attractive, peaceful rooms (n° 20 has a view of the Duomo). Young, friendly staff. 70–90 €.

Pensione Bandini (**E** D2)
→ Piazza Santo Spirito, 9
Tel. 055 21 53 08
Honeymoon suites on the upper floors of the exquisite Guadagni palace (15th–16th century). You can chill out on the loggia-terrace above the square.
76–112 €. No credit cards.

Maxim (**A** B2)
→ Via dei Calzaiuoli, 11b
Tel. 055 217 474
This well-situated hotel is close to the Duomo. It has a friendly atmosphere with cheerful paintings by the proprietor on the walls and around 30 rooms, over-looking the quiet courtyard or the street and the Duomo (if you lean out of the window). Some

AIRPORT

Aeroporto A. Vespucci
(5 miles west of Florence)
→ Tel. 055 37 34 98
Lost Luggage
→ Tel. 055 30 80 23
Links with the city center
→ 'Vola in bus' to S. M.
Novella, every 30 mins
(3.10 €)
→ Taxi, 20 mins (13–15 €)
Flights & reservations
From the UK:
Alitalia
→ Tel. 08705 448 259
BritishAirways
→ Tel. 0845 77 333 77
From the US:
Alitalia
→ Tel. 1 800 223 5730
American Airlines
→ Tel. 1 800 433 7300

AIRPORT AND ROAD ACCESS

---

*Unless otherwise stated,
the prices given here are
for a double room. They
vary depending on the
season, the amenities
(private bathroom, TV, air
conditioning) and the
length of stay (negotiable).
Credit cards are often not
accepted.*

RESERVATIONS

It is highly advisable to
book several months in
advance. If not, as soon
as you arrive at the station,
go to the reservation office
but there is a charge for
this service and there are
often long queues.

UNDER 50 €

Camping Michelangelo
(F E3)
→ Viale Michelangiolo, 80
Tel. 055 681 19 77. Bus 13
A wonderful view over the
city and a comprehensive

range of facilities. There
are only two drawbacks:
the lack of shade and
some noise near the road.
Site 4.80 € + 7.50 €/person
Villa Camerata
→ Viale Augusto Righi, 2-4
Tel. 055 60 14 51
Bus 17-a/b
One of the most beautiful
youth hostels in Europe,
30 mins from the city. 15 €.
Ostello Santa Monaca
(E D2)
→ Via Santa Monaca, 6
Tel. 055 23 83 38
Between Santa Maria del
Carmine and Santo
Spirito, this hostel has
dormitories with bunk
beds (not mixed) and the
feel of a university
residence. Bed 15 €.
Istituto Gould (E D2)
→ Via dei Serragli, 49
Tel. 055 23 83 38
Mon-Fri 9am–1pm, 3–7pm;
Sat 9am–1pm
Clean rooms (one to four
beds), reminiscent of a

girl's boarding school (not
mixed). Bed 20–35 €.
Istituto Pio X (E D2)
→ Via dei Serragli, 104
Tel. 055 22 50 44
Quiet refuge overlooking a
courtyard, run by monks.
Rooms with three to seven
beds. Bed 13–16 €.
Aily Home (A A5)
→ Piazza Santo Stefano, 81
Tel. 055 239 65 05
Four simple rooms (ask
for the one with a view of
the square) and a warm
reception from the elderly
owner. No private bath-
room, no breakfast. 40 €.
Ostello Archi Rossi (B F1)
→ Via Faenza, 94r
Tel. 055 29 08 04
Closed 11am–2.30pm and
1am. Two rooms have
disabled access
Near the station, in a row
of cheap hotels, this well-
established hostel is
popular with students.
Rooms with one to nine
beds overlooking a

pedestrianized stre
or a tree-lined court
Friendly reception.
Internet access. 16–

50–77 €

**Suore Oblate
dell'Assunzione** (
→ Borgo Pinti, 15
Tel. 055 248 05 82/3
Decent rooms with
one to three beds in
Renaissance palace
nuns: wonderful ga
and an oasis of pea
and quiet. No break
Doors close at 11.30
Bed 34 € (68 € for t
**Casa Santo Nome
di Gesù** (E C1)
→ Piazza del Carmir
Tel. 055 21 38 56
Delightful accommo
with the Franciscan
on the left bank of t
Arno: lovely garden
15th-century palace
Curfew at 11.30pm.
Bed 30 € (60 € for t

Transports in Florence

| | Terminus |
| | Line number |

SAN JACOPINO

CANALE MACINATE

FORTEZZA DA BASSO

LE CASCINE

LE CASCINE

STAZIONE F.S.
PORTA AL PRATO

STAZ. CENTRALE F.S.
SANTA MARIA
NOVELLA

S. LORENZO

S. MARIA
NOVELLA

S. MARIA
NOVELLA

FIUME ARNO

OGNISSANTI

PIGNONE

S. FREDIANO
IN CESTELLO

MONTICELLI

SAN FREDIANO

SANTA MARIA
DEL CARMINE

SANTO
SPIRITO

SANTO SPIRITO

PALAZZO
PITTI

GIARDINO
TORRIGIANI

GIARDINO
DI
BOBOLI

GALLUZZO

SCOOTERS IN FLORENCE

the lavishly restored former Hotel Splendor, deserves its name, which translates as: 'The garden of the Medici'. All mod cons, marvelous panoramic views and a flower-filled terrace for breakfast in the sun: an oasis just a short walk from San Marco. 163–180 €.

David (**F** F2)
→ Viale Michelangelo, 1
Tel. 055 681 16 95
www.davidhotel.com
This comfortable 19th-century villa with the feel of a family-owned guesthouse has been handed down through the generations and is extremely well run. Well-kept rooms and period furniture. With its own parking lot and garden-terrace. 150–186 €.

Torre Guelfa (**B** F4)
→ Borgo Santi Apostoli, 8
Tel. 055 239 63 38
This 13th-century tower

harks back to the cruel days of the Guelphs (supporters of the pope) who defeated the Ghibellines (supporters of the emperor): 15 fairy-tale rooms with a canopy bed. Elegant service. Bar on the top floor with panoramic terrace (March-Oct). 170 €.

EXPENSIVE ...

Monna Lisa (**D** B2)
→ Borgo Pinti, 27
Tel. 055 24 79 751
www.monnalisa.it
The unassuming façade of this Renaissance palazzo hides a hotel of great charm, with wooden ceilings, cotto (terracotta) floors, works of art and antiques (the bar is an old confessional). Ask for a room looking out onto the hotel's greatest asset: a gorgeous garden where breakfast is served in summer. 180–284 €

Torre di Bellosguardo (**E** A3)
→ Via Roti de Michelozzi, 2
Tel. 055 229 81 45
A 15-minute drive from the center, this 16th-century villa, built around a tower, is a haven of cool in hot summer days. Spacious, tasteful, with beautiful reception rooms and bedrooms, ornamental gardens and a swimming pool, staying here is a must. Amazing 360° panoramic views from the top-floor suites. Car essential. 280 €.

Gallery Art Hotel (**B** C2)
→ Vicolo dell'Oro, 5
Tel. 055 27263
www.lungarnohotels.com
Launched by the Salvatore Ferragamo fashion group, this hotel, doubling as an art gallery for contemporary artists, oozes class and slick chic. Moving around leather, wood, wool and stone you become the hero of a design book. 310 €.

TAXIS

Official taxis are white, with a sign on the roof.
Taxi stands
Stazione, Santa Trinità, Repubblica, Santa Maria Novella, Duomo, San Marco, Santa Croce.
Radiotaxis
→ Tel. 055 42 42/47 98, 43 90/43 86

Fares
→ 5–8 € per journey

CARS

You are only allowed to drive and park in the historic center to get to your hotel. Be warned: there is a highly efficient towing service in operation in the city.
→ Tel. 055 30 82 49
Parking lots
Public parking lots charge less than hotel garages if you are staying for several days.
→ Piazza della Libertà, Piazza Stazione, Fortezza da Basso, Porta Romana...
Car hire
Avis (**B** D3)
→ Borgo Ognissanti, 128r. Tel. 055 239 88 26
Europcar (**B** D3)
→ Borgo Ognissanti, 53
Tel. 055 236 00 72
Hertz (**B** D3)
→ Via Finiguerra, 33r
Tel. 055 28 22 60

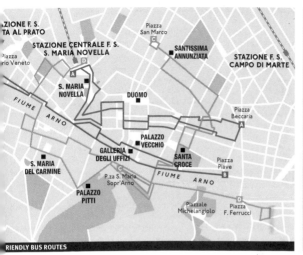

RIENDLY BUS ROUTES

BIKES

Bikes and scooters are a popular mode of transport in Florence and the nicest way to explore the city center or further afield. Hire a 125cc for fun-filled sightseeing.

Bike hire

Alinari
→ *Via Guelfa, 85r* (**C** A3)
Tel. 055 28 05 00
Bikes and scooters.

Florence by bike
→ *Via San Zanobi, 120/122r* (**C** B2). *Tel. 055 48 89 92*
Bikes and scooters, guided tours.

Happy Rent (**B** D3)
→ *Borgo Ognissanti, 153r*
Tel. 055 239 96 96
Scooters, cars.

---

s have double-glazing.
09 €.

Agape (**F** D4)
a Torre del Gallo 8/10
55 22 00 44/233 70 12
bus 12 or 13 then
8 to this gorgeous
e run by nuns, far
the bustle of the city,
bove San Miniato.
illa looks out onto
den full of boxwood
, cypresses and an
grove. Free parking.
er available. 100 €.

giorno Pergola (**D** B2)
a della Pergola, 23
55 21 38 86
well-equipped
o apartments for long
, often used by the
cians and actors from
eater opposite. 100 €.

–130 €

etini (**A** A1)
a de' Conti, 7
55 21 35 61/28 29 80
ful, cozy rooms, a

minute-walk from Michelangelo and San Lorenzo. Both décor and staff are stylish: this contributes to a very pleasant stay. 124–150 €.

Albergo la Scaletta (**E** F2)
→ *Via Guicciardini, 13*
Tel. 055 283 028/214 255
Exceptional location: the terraces on the top floor of this 15th-century hotel afford a view of the Boboli Garden and the rooftops. Each of the exquisitely decorated rooms has its own character. Breakfast included. 125 €.

Pensione Annalena (**E** D3)
→ *Via Romana, 34*
Tel. 055 22 24 02/96 00
Opposite the most unobtrusive entrance to the Boboli Garden, this 16th-century palace with its faded façade, has balconies overlooking the gardens and 22 tasteful rooms. 120–159 €.

130–155 €
Aprile (**B** E3)
→ *Via della Scala, 6*
Tel. 055 216 237
All the beauty of a romantic palace. Every room has its own distinctive style. Some are decorated with frescos. Rooms either have a view of Santa Maria Novella, the garden or the terrace. Special deals when staying two to three days in low season. 130–170 €.

Burchianti (**B** F3)
→ *Via Giglio, 8*
Tel. 055 21 27 96
Sweet dreams come as standard in the frescoed rooms of this stately 16th-century residence, which has recently been given a makeover. 140 €.

Alessandra (**B** F4)
→ *Borgo Santi Apostoli, 17*
Tel. 055 283 438
Rooms with classical décor and fine views over the church square (n° 10), of the Arno river (n° 22 or

n° 5), or simply of the peaceful street. 100–145 €.

Casci (**C** B3)
→ *Via Cavour, 13*
Tel. 055 211 686
Friendly, family-owned hotel, between the Duomo and San Marco. Decent rooms overlooking the courtyard or the street (double-glazing). Large breakfast. 90–135 €.

California (**C** B4)
→ *Via Ricasoli, 30*
Tel. 055 28 34 99/27 53
Peace and quiet and all mod cons in red rooms done out in satin, ivory and wood, with marble bathroom. N° 123 has a view of the Duomo. Breakfast (buffet) on the terrace. 90–150 €.

155–190 €

Orto de'Medici (**C** B3)
→ *Via San Gallo, 30*
Tel. 055 48 34 27
This 19th-century residence,

Letters **(A, B, C...)** relate to the matching sections. Letters on their own refer to the spread with the useful addresses. Letters followed by a star **(A★)** refer to the spread with the fold-out map and the places to visit. The number **(1)** refers to the double page **Welcome to Florence!** at the beginning of this guide.